Building Character & Community in the Classroom

Written by
Rick DuVall

Editor:
Joellyn Thrall Cicciarelli

Illustrator:
Darcy Tom

Project Director:
Carolea Williams

Photo of boy holding bird provided by The Image Bank

Table of Contents

Introduction

A caring classroom community consists of happy, confident students led by a strong, nurturing teacher. *Building Character and Community in the Classroom* offers creative activities to build a sense of community among your students through the development of positive character traits. The activities offer fun and meaningful ways for students to become part of a positive classroom community—caring for one another and developing into socially-responsible individuals.

Why Is Classroom Community Important?

A sense of community was, at one time, more a part of life in our society. Out of necessity, people would come together to help one another. Caring and sharing were natural components of daily life. However, in today's society, these traits are sometimes replaced by individualism and competition.

Today's children witness violence on television, in the movies, and, more tragically, in their neighborhoods and homes. Many are victims of abuse and neglect. As a result, too many children are not a part of a caring community in their daily lives.

As our students grow up, they will face a very competitive job market. Our society has moved from the Industrial Age into the Information Age. Workers are required to possess critical thinking skills as well as skills in cooperation and collaboration. The structure of the workplace, in addition to a changing population, requires workers to cooperate with one another, understanding and respecting diverse groups of people.

For many children, a safe, happy, caring classroom environment is the starting point toward a bright future. As students learn to care and develop positive character traits, they experience success both academically and socially. Success breeds success. Forming happy, socially-responsible children should be the goal of every parent and teacher. Our future depends on it.

What Does a Classroom Community Look Like?

As members of a classroom community, students really know one another. They feel they belong. Students know they are cared for and are expected to care for others. Each day, students share the responsibility for achieving common goals.

Respect is highlighted and demonstrated in a caring classroom community. Students are concerned about everyone's welfare. They encourage one another. Students are involved in making important decisions that affect the classroom community.

Teachers have clear expectations for student work and behavior. Teachers and students view mistakes as a natural part of the learning process and not as a sign of failure. Students are viewed as responsible learners and are treated equitably. They collaborate on schoolwork for better understanding.

Students celebrate the diversity of individual skills and talents brought to their classroom. They feel the support and security that comes from being part of a close-knit group. At the same time, students retain their individuality, feeling free to differ from one another.

What Are the Rights of Learners in a Classroom Community?

All members of a community have certain rights. A classroom community is no different. To ensure positive growth both academically and socially, keep in mind 12 basic rights students have in a caring classroom community. Children in a caring classroom community have a right to . . .

- be personally greeted and welcomed into the classroom each day.
- be challenged by a rigorous curriculum that helps them develop to their full potential.
- frequently cooperate and collaborate with their peers.
- socialize with their friends.
- choose learning activities.
- enjoy themselves each day.
- make mistakes without receiving criticism.
- be respected by their peers and teacher.
- be involved in critical decisions that affect their classroom community.
- talk and listen to one another.
- ask for assistance when needed and receive it.
- be safe physically and emotionally.

When teachers work to protect these basic rights, a caring, socially-responsible community of learners results.

Getting Started

Through the use of character-building definitions, posters, and activities, your students will become teammates, learning partners, and best of all, trusted friends. Each character-building section begins with a definition of the character trait, a list of practical applications of that trait, and a poster idea. Enlarge, decorate, and display the posters to remind students of their character-building efforts.

Consider one of the following models as you plan to incorporate character- and community-building activities into your curriculum.

Character Trait of the Month

Devote one full month to the development of a specific character trait such as respect, compassion, kindness, friendship, self-discipline, honesty, trust, or responsibility. Center activities and discussion around the character trait, integrating it into the curriculum.

The "T.V. Commercial" Method

Use activities from a variety of chapters (like short commercials that appeal to short attention spans), concentrating on several character traits at a time. After each activity, explain or have students guess which character trait was the focus of the activity.

Pick and Choose

After observing your students the first month of school, determine which character traits they need to develop most. Concentrate on those traits first, teaching other character traits after your students have made progress.

School-Wide Program

Choose a character trait to highlight for one week. Invite all staff, including physical education, music, and art teachers to use activities from a chapter. Ask the principal to hold a character-trait assembly in which classes perform skits, give presentations, or relay special announcements. Have every class make and hang posters highlighting the character trait. Have grade-level teachers meet and choose activities to complete simultaneously.

After you have decided how to structure your character-building program, use the activity ideas presented in this book as a first step toward establishing a cohesive unit of students working together toward a common goal.

MATERIALS

Preamble and Bill of Rights of the U.S. Constitution

light brown butcher or parchment paper

markers

Class Bill of Rights and Responsibilities

Read aloud the Preamble to the U.S. Constitution and Bill of Rights. Discuss their historical significance and interpret their meaning. Together, brainstorm a class "preamble." Write the new preamble on light brown butcher or parchment paper. Use the Preamble to the Constitution as a model. For example:

We, the people of Room 21, in order to form a more perfect classroom community, establish justice, ensure caring and tranquility, provide for common respect, promote peace and understanding, and secure the blessing of happiness and collaboration for ourselves and our visitors, do ordain and establish this Bill of Rights and Responsibilities for the Dreamers. (For an explanation of *Dreamers,* see Naming the Class, page 7.)

Divide the class into small groups and ask them to brainstorm rights they believe they should have in the classroom. As a class, discuss each list and decide which rights the entire community believes they should have. Explain that with rights come responsibilities. For example, if students believe they have the *right* to be safe in their classroom, then they have the *responsibility* to never touch anyone in anger. Next, ask groups to list responsibilities required of them to secure the rights established by the class. Have each group share their list. Decide which responsibilities the class can accept. Copy the rights and responsibilities on light brown butcher or parchment paper and display them in the classroom. Have each student sign the chart. Send the rights and responsibilities home so parents know the community's expectations.

Class T-Shirt

MATERIALS

students' favorite T-shirts

plain T-shirts

fabric paints

Hold a Community T-Shirt Day, asking students to wear their favorite T-shirts that advertise a community or organization. For example, students might wear a shirt depicting their favorite sports team, university, church, school, or summer camp. (Be sure to wear one, too!) Have a T-shirt fashion show, allowing each student to model and discuss his or her T-shirt. Compare the shirts and discuss their common elements. Divide students into small groups and ask them to design a T-shirt for their classroom community. Invite groups to share their designs and discuss positive aspects of each shirt. Have the class choose a favorite element from each group and combine them into one design. Invite students to duplicate the design on blank T-shirts using fabric paint. Agree on a day for all classroom community members to wear their shirts, such as every Friday. Students can also wear their shirts on field trips and during special events and assemblies.

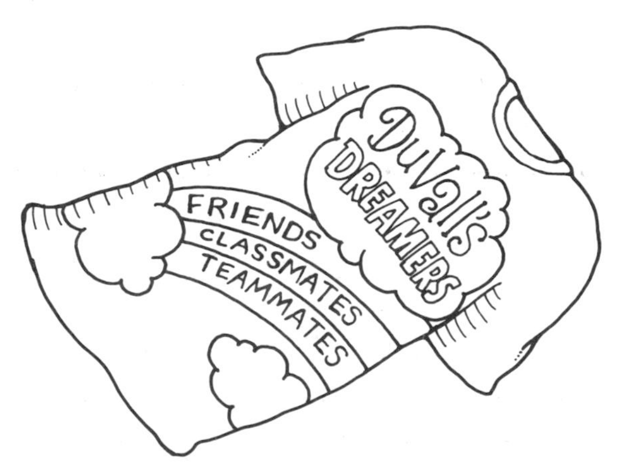

Naming the Class

MATERIALS

none

As a class, brainstorm group identities such as the Chicago Bears, University of Kentucky Wildcats, or Greenpeace. Discuss the desire to establish a common identity for your class, emphasizing that the group name should be positive. (Miller's Meanies would not be acceptable.) Provide a few examples to get students thinking, such as a play on your last name (General's Soldiers or Street's Lights) or an alliteration (DuVall's Dreamers). Place students in small groups to brainstorm possible names. Bring the class back together and compile a list of suggestions. Discuss the suggestions and decide upon one name. Use the name routinely when referring to the class (e.g., *Good morning, Stars!).* Using the name, develop a few cheers or chants for test preparation and other times when motivation is needed.

MATERIALS

stuffed animal or puppet

tote bag

blank journal

Class Mascot and Journal

Bring in a stuffed animal, puppet, or other object that characterizes the class name. Place the mascot and a blank journal in a tote bag. Tell students they will have an opportunity to take the mascot home and write about their experiences with it. To model, take the mascot home first. Write a rich, detailed, humorous story chronicling your experiences together. Share the story with the class. Invite each child to take the mascot and journal home. Be sure to provide plenty of time for students to read their stories aloud.

MATERIALS

flags or flag pictures

colored construction paper

crayons, colored pencils, markers, paint

colored felt

glue

Class Flag

Display flags from countries, states, and corporations. Discuss the symbolism associated with each flag. Ask each student to use art supplies and design a flag for the classroom community. Display students' work and discuss each flag's elements. Divide the class into groups of four to design another flag. Have groups incorporate elements from individual student flags. Display the new flags and, as a community, decide which flag will symbolize the classroom community. Invite volunteers to duplicate that flag using felt and glue. Display the new flag in the classroom. Invite a student volunteer to carry the flag at school functions such as assemblies and Track and Field Day.

Friendship Circle

MATERIALS

yarn or Koosh ball

Divide a section of chalkboard into four columns. Label the first column *Sharing*, the second *Compliments* (writing *I thank . . . , I commend . . . , I appreciate . . . ,* and *I applaud . . .* underneath), the third *Solutions*, and the fourth *Funnies*. Throughout the week, have volunteers sign up under a column so they can speak during Friendship Circle that week. (Students should sign up for one column only.)

Those who sign up for Sharing share anything they want to communicate to the rest of the class. Students who sign up for Compliments give specific praise to a classmate. If a compliment is vague, such as *Thanks, Gene, for being my friend,* respond with, *How does Gene show you that he's your friend?* Through this process, students learn to comfortably express their feelings. Students who sign up for Solutions have tried to solve a problem peacefully and cannot resolve it. Students share the problem and the unsuccessfully-attempted solutions so the rest of the class can offer advice. When a new possible solution is chosen, the community decides if they need to follow up on it. If so, make a note on the board to remind the class to revisit the problem during the next Friendship Circle. Students who sign up for Funnies tell jokes, riddles, or puns.

Conduct Friendship Circle at the same time each week. Have students sit in a circle (joining hands, if you wish). Appoint a leader to begin singing a friendship song or read a poem as the official opening. Invite other students to join in. Have the leader pass the yarn or Koosh ball to the first person who signed up for Sharing. Only the person holding the ball is allowed to speak. Everyone else is expected to listen with their eyes, ears, and hearts (see page 28). After Sharing students have spoken, the ball is passed to the first person who signed up for Compliments. When the ball has been passed to everyone who wants to give compliments, it is passed to the first person who signed up for Solutions. When all solutions have been discussed, Friendship Circle ends on an up-beat note with Funnies. To close, have the class join hands and sing another friendship song.

MATERIALS

none

Closing Circle

Complete this activity approximately ten minutes before dismissal. Each day, ask a different question, inviting each student to respond. (Allow students to pass if they do not wish to share.) For example, on Monday, ask students to share a highlight from their weekend. On Tuesday, ask students a hypothetical question such as *What would be the first thing you would do if you suddenly won a million dollars?* On Wednesday, ask students to evaluate an element of the class about which you need feedback, such as *What part of long division gives you the most trouble?* On Thursday, ask students to share their favorite lesson from the week. On Friday, name a Student of the Week and ask each member of the class to share one thing they like about him or her.

MATERIALS

chart paper

markers

Getting to Know You

Complete this activity at the beginning of the year. On chart paper, write interview questions such as *What is your name? How old are you? Where were you born? What is one thing you want everyone to know about you? Whom do you admire? What is your favorite pastime? What do you like most about school?* Have students find partners. Ask each student to take ten minutes and interview his or her partner, finding out information from the list, and asking any additional questions he or she wishes. Have the class form a large circle. Invite each student to share the information he or she learned about his or her partner.

Self-Esteem

a sense of one's own dignity and worth

Poster Idea

Enlarge, decorate, and display the following poster to build students' self-esteem.

Children with self-esteem are easy to spot in a classroom setting. A sense of security and self-trust surrounds them. Specifically, students with self-esteem

- smile, laugh, and tell jokes.
- share information and stories about themselves.
- happily offer help to others.
- forgive themselves for mistakes.
- have patience with themselves and others.
- enjoy having their work displayed.
- work well alone and in groups.
- volunteer in class.
- know and share their talents.
- enjoy being unique.

MATERIALS

The Sneetches by Dr. Seuss

drawing paper

crayons, colored pencils, markers

Celebrating Diversity

Display the cover of *The Sneetches*. Ask students to predict what the star on the characters' bellies symbolizes. Read the story aloud. Discuss student reactions to the story. Have students speculate what the world would be like if everyone were the same. Have each student draw a unique creature to celebrate diversity. Under the pictures, have students write one thing that makes their characters unique. Display the characters on a bulletin board under the heading *Always Be Yourself!*

MATERIALS

Be Good to Eddie Lee by Virginia Fleming

Appreciating Others' Unique Qualities

Discuss experiences students have had when encountering people different from themselves. Ask students to share how they handled these situations. Display the cover of *Be Good to Eddie Lee*. Ask students to predict the story's plot. Read the story aloud. Discuss student reactions to the book. Emphasize that while Eddie Lee had noticeable differences from his peers, he had special abilities that others did not. One at a time, read each student's name. Invite a volunteer to state a positive, unique quality each student possesses.

Stand if You Can . . .

In advance, write a list of several "stand-if-you-can" sentences that describe accomplishments, such as *Stand if you can stand on your head; Stand if you can count to ten in two different languages; Stand if you can whistle a song; Stand if you can say the alphabet backward.* Ask the class to sit in chairs in a large circle. Read the stand-if-you-can statements aloud. Have students stand if they can do the things described in the sentences. After reading the sentences, have students discuss how they felt when they acknowledged themselves for their accomplishments. Explain that part of being a friend to yourself is recognizing your talents.

MATERIALS

writing paper

Giving a Hand

Ask students to trace one of their hands on a piece of tagboard. Have them paint the hands with watercolors and cut them out. Ask students to brainstorm five positive attributes they possess. Have them list one characteristic on each finger of their hand cutouts. To display, join the hands in pairs as if they are ready to shake hands.

MATERIALS

tagboard

pencils, pens, crayons, colored pencils, markers

watercolors, paintbrushes

scissors

glue

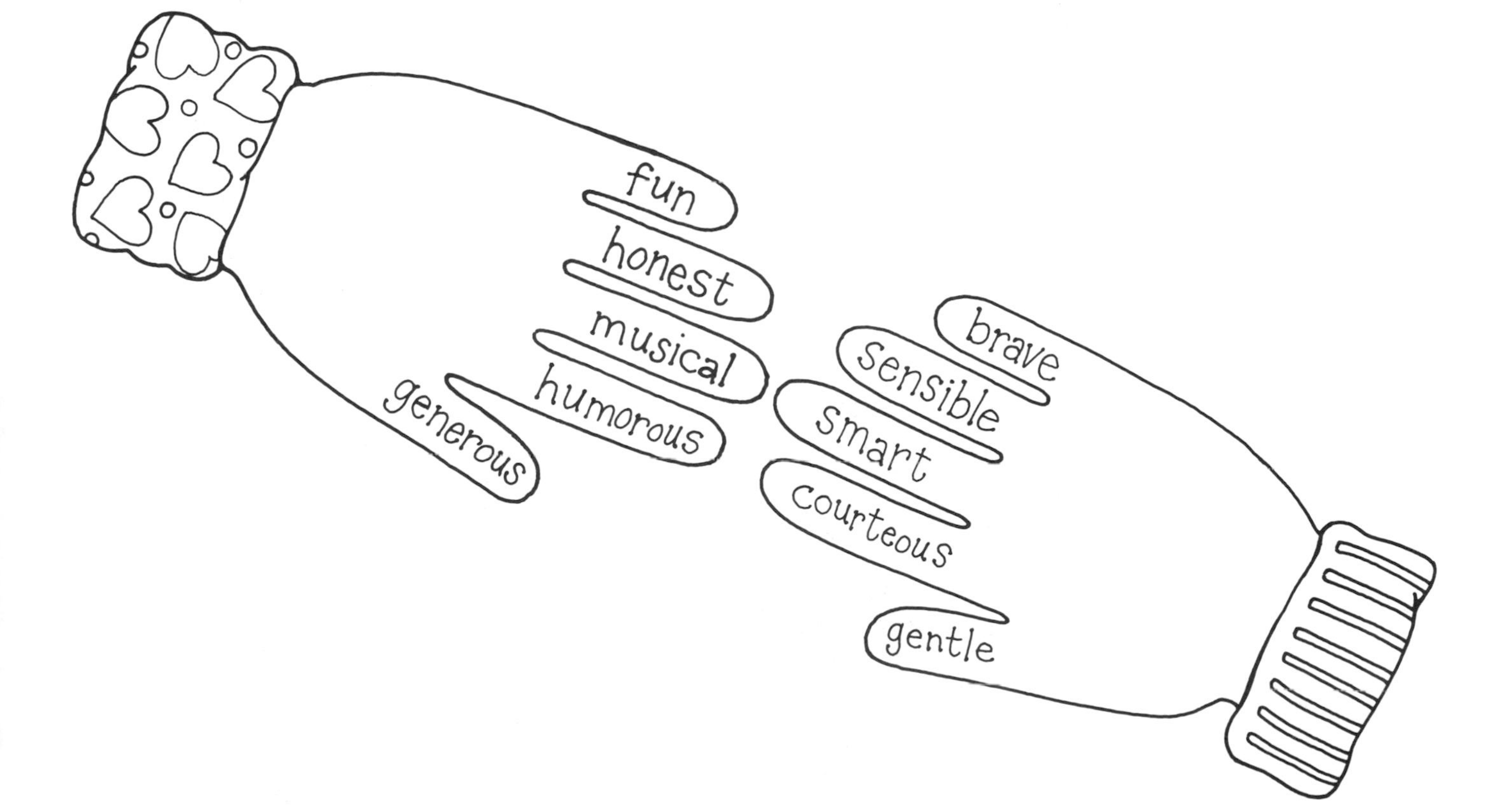

MATERIALS

writing paper

The Important Book by Margaret Wise Brown

Important Me!

Ask students to list things that make them special. Read *The Important Book* aloud. Have students use the word pattern from the book to create a list of things that make them important. Explain that part of trusting yourself is having confidence in yourself and your abilities. Combine student work into a class book entitled *The Important Class*.

MATERIALS

construction paper

pencils, crayons, colored pencils, markers

Name Game

Have students hold construction paper vertically and write and decorate each letter of his or her name down the left side of the paper. Next to each letter, have students write a positive adjective that describes them and begins with that letter, such as *Caring, Athletic, Respectful, Adorable*. Divide the class into groups. Invite students to share their names and adjectives with their group.

I'm Proud

MATERIALS

none

Invite the class to sit in a large circle. Taking turns, have each student complete the sentence *I'm proud I can . . . .* After all students have spoken, have them complete the sentence *I'm proud to be . . . .*

Valuing Your Name

MATERIALS

My Name Is Maria Isabel by Alma Flor Ada

name tags

markers

Read aloud *My Name Is Maria Isabel.* At the end of the day, ask students to go home and interview their parents about the history of their first and last names. Have them ask questions such as *Why was I given my name? Did you consider any other names? What were they? What nationality is my last name? What does it mean?* The next day, invite students to share their findings. For extra fun, have each student choose a new first name for him- or herself and write it on a name tag. Invite students to tell why they chose their names and wear them for an hour. Have students call each other by their new names for that hour as well.

MATERIALS

All I Am by Eileen Roe

writing paper

crayons, colored pencils, markers

construction-paper book covers

drawing paper

This Is Me

Divide the class into pairs. Ask partners to honestly describe themselves to each other, sharing both positive and negative attributes. Read *All I Am* aloud. Have students follow the book's format and use drawing paper to create their own "All-I-Am" books with construction-paper covers. Keep the books for sharing during parent/teacher conferences.

MATERIALS

4" x 6" index cards

Who Am I?

Give each student an index card and have him or her follow these directions: *In the top left corner of the card, write one thing you do well at home. In the top right corner of the card, write one thing people admire about you. In the bottom left corner of the card, write one thing you do well at school. In the bottom right corner of the card, write one thing you like about your appearance. In the center of the card, write one thing you like about your personality.* Divide the class into pairs. Invite students to share cards with their partners.

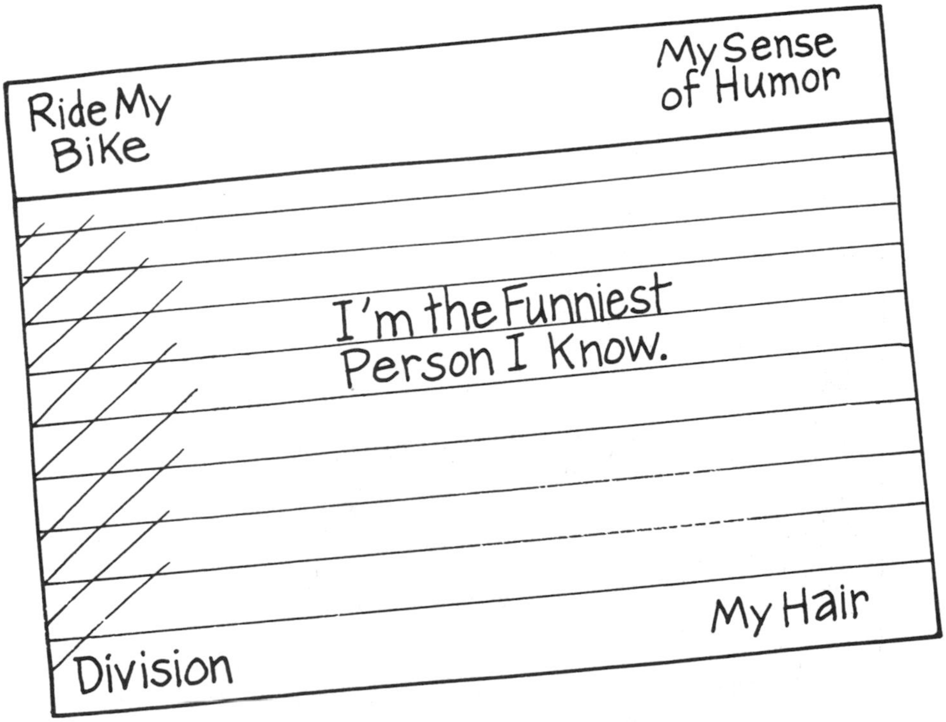

I Like Me!

Ask students to share something they like about themselves. Read aloud *All About Stacy.* Ask students to write or draw all the things they like about themselves. Explain that part of trusting in yourself is showing pride in your own abilities. Go around the room and have students complete the sentence *I like me because I . . . .*

MATERIALS

All About Stacy by Patricia R. Giff

writing or drawing paper

pencils, crayons, colored pencils, markers

Me Maps

Distribute materials and invite students to make Me Maps—maps that begin with students' dates and places of birth and lead a trail to the present, showing places students have been and experiences they have had throughout their lives. After the maps are made, divide the class into groups. Remind the class to listen with their eyes, ears, and hearts (see page 28). Have each student share his or her map with the group.

MATERIALS

butcher or drawing paper

crayons, colored pencils, markers

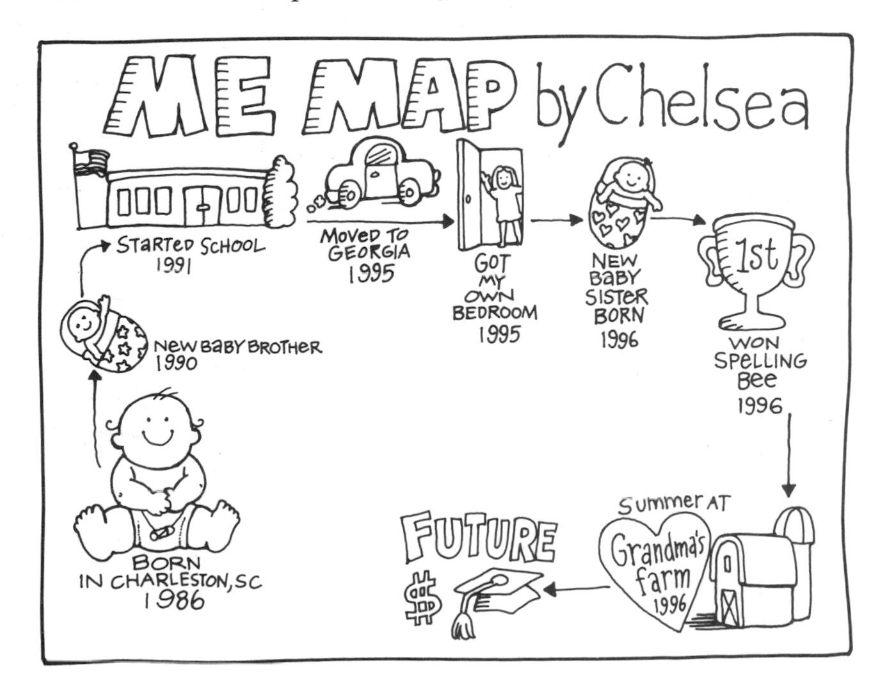

MATERIALS

none

Move if You . . .

Have students sit in chairs in a large circle. Stand in the center and say a sentence such as *Move if you have eaten ice cream this week.* At this signal, everyone who has eaten ice cream, including you, scrambles to find a new chair. The person who did not find a chair must go to the center and think of a new "move-if-you" sentence. If students have trouble thinking of a sentence, whisper examples to them, such as *Move if you can run fast; Move if you have a dog; Move if you like baseball;* or *Move if you like to use a computer.* After several rounds, have students discuss how everyone is unique and has special talents and interests.

MATERIALS

lyrics and recording of "My Favorite Things" (from the soundtrack of *The Sound of Music*)

record, cassette, or compact disc player

drawing paper

stapler, book-binding machine, or three-ring binder

My Favorite Things

Play "My Favorite Things." Ask each student to think of one favorite thing and share it with the class. (If a student duplicates another student's favorite thing, ask him or her to share their second favorite thing.) As each student shares, write his or her favorite thing at the top of a separate sheet of drawing paper that says, *I like . . . .* Display the papers on tables. Invite students to walk around the tables and sign their names on any page that describes something they like. Discuss how everyone in the class has at least one interest they share with other members of the class. Bind papers into a book and add it to your classroom library.

Unconditional Love

MATERIALS

The Gift of the Magi by O. Henry

construction-paper strips

crayons, colored pencils, markers

glue

Ask students if they have ever doubted someone's love or friendship. Invite students to share their experiences. Display the cover of *The Gift of the Magi.* Ask students to predict what the story is about and where it takes place. Read the book aloud. Ask students to think of ways their relatives show them love. Have students write each way their relatives show love on individual construction-paper strips. Invite students to use as many strips as they wish. Have the class glue their strips into interlocking loops to create a large paper chain. Decorate the classroom with the chain. Above the chain, hang a banner saying, *The Chain of Love Can't Be Broken.*

Taking Pride in Your Heritage

MATERIALS

The Black Snowman by Phil Mendez

large world map

small stickers

Ask students to share memories about enjoying winter weather. Discuss elements that make these events memorable, such as spending time with family and friends. Display the cover of *The Black Snowman.* Ask students to observe the illustrator's use of color. Read the book aloud. Ask students to share what they know about their heritage. Have each student find out about his or her family background and the name of a country in which his or her ancestors lived. The next day, invite volunteers to share what they learned. Find each volunteer's countries of heritage on a world map, and invite him or her to place a sticker on each country. Have students who choose not to share place a sticker on the United States. (Some students may not know about their heritage or may have forgotten to ask their parents.) Discuss the diversity and similarities represented by the stickers.

MATERIALS

yellow construction paper

crayons, colored pencils, markers

three-ring binder

Class Yellow Pages

Early in the school year, choose one talent each student possesses, such as *knows multiplication tables, is a great speller, can draw animals, is a terrific baseball player,* or *always listens to friends.* Announce each student's area of expertise. Tell students that throughout the year, they will be called upon to help their classmates in their area of expertise. Explain that their names and talents will be advertised in a Class Yellow Pages, similar to those in the telephone directory. As a class, examine the Yellow Pages in a telephone directory. Give students yellow paper, and have them design an advertisement for their talents. Place the advertisements in alphabetical order according to talent in a three-ring binder. Display the Yellow Pages in a prominent place in the classroom for easy reference.

MATERIALS

notebooks (with red, blue, green, orange, and yellow covers)

Dialogue Journals

Distribute a notebook to each student. Explain that the notebooks will be journals. Tell students that red journals will be collected on Monday, blue on Tuesday, green on Wednesday, orange on Thursday, and yellow on Friday. Each morning, have all students write an entry, but have students with the designated color write an entry to you about something they want to discuss. (Do not correct or grade entries. Instead, use them as a means for you and your students to get to know each other.) Collect the designated journals after school and respond to each with one or two sentences. Use your responses to answer questions and model correct spelling, punctuation, sentence formation, capitalization, and other writing skills.

Respect

showing others consideration, admiration, and honor

Poster Idea

Enlarge, decorate, and display the following poster to remind students how to show respect.

A classroom of respectful children—a wonderful thought—and for many teachers, a wonderful reality. In school, children with respect

- listen.
- keep unkind thoughts to themselves.
- speak kindly to teachers and other students.
- play fairly.
- wait their turn.
- raise their hands before talking.
- say *please* and *thank you.*
- clean up after themselves.
- share.

MATERIALS

The Three Astronauts by Umberto Eco and Eugenio Carmi

red, yellow, and blue tempera paint

paintbrushes

drawing paper

Racial Harmony

Discuss stereotypes, suggesting that many people judge all members of a group based on the actions and/or appearance of a segment of that group. Ask students to think how a visitor from another planet might stereotype Earthlings if it only met one or two people. Ask questions such as *When the alien returned to his planet, how would he describe a typical Earthling? How tall are Earthlings? What color is their skin? What color is their hair and eyes? What behaviors and actions exemplify Earthlings?* and *What is the approximate age of Earthlings?* Read *The Three Astronauts* aloud. Invite students to reflect upon what the three astronauts learned during their visit to another planet. Give each student red, yellow, and blue paint and a piece of paper. Explain that these are the primary colors and that all other colors are created by combining them. Ask students to place a dab of each paint on paper. Ask them to mix their colors slowly for five seconds. Have students compare their blended colors, discussing differences in the final results. Use the paint as an analogy to explain the fallacy of stereotypes. Discuss how all the paints looked the same in the beginning, but were different in the end. Explain that like the paint, people may look the same, but are really unique and different.

MATERIALS

class lists

We're Alike, We're Different

Distribute a class list to each student. Divide the class into pairs. Have partners list three things they have in common with each other. Next, ask them to list three differences. At a signal, have students check off their partner's name and quickly find a new partner. Repeat the activity. Continue switching and sharing until students have spoken with everyone.

Challenge Hour

MATERIALS

The Balancing Girl by Bernice Rabe

blindfolds

mittens

straws

Discuss times when students had to overcome adversity. Display the cover of *The Balancing Girl.* Have students make predictions about the story's plot. Read the book aloud. For a week, designate one hour each day to be Challenge Hour. On Monday, have no speaking for an hour. On Tuesday, have students wear blindfolds for an hour. On Wednesday, have students wear a mitten on their writing hand for an hour. On Thursday, have students hop around on one leg for an hour. On Friday, have students breathe through straws for an hour. At the end of each hour, have students discuss their frustrations, embarrassments, and feelings about having these physical challenges. Have students discuss how they will think or behave differently when seeing or meeting a person with a physical challenge.

Looks Like, Sounds Like

MATERIALS

chart paper

markers

Write *respect* on the top of a chart. Create a two-column chart labeled *Looks Like* on the left and *Sounds Like* on the right. Have students brainstorm ideas for the two columns. Post the chart. Whenever students work in groups, watch for the sights and sounds of respect. After students finish group work, acknowledge examples you witnessed.

RESPECT

LOOKS LIKE	SOUNDS LIKE
· helping others · hands to yourself · friendly faces	· quiet voices · kind words · friendly laughter · "please" and "thank you"

MATERIALS

chart paper

markers

Officer, Officer!

As a class, discuss a police officer's job description. On chart paper, list a police officer's duties. Ask students to refer to the duties and tell why a police officer's job is so difficult. Divide the class into groups. Have each group choose one duty (that involves dealing with people) and create a skit showing a police officer in action. The skit should show people treating the officer with respect. After all skits have been performed, ask students why it is important to treat police officers with respect. Invite a police officer to class to discuss his or her job, telling students how police officers feel when citizens respect and disrespect them. To close, have the officer compare his or her duties with the class list.

MATERIALS

Blubber by Judy Blume

Valuing Others

Ask students to share times they felt put down by others. Display the cover of the book *Blubber.* Ask students to describe what appears to be happening on the cover. Have students predict how they think Linda feels about her nickname. Read the book aloud. Have students brainstorm what they can do the next time they are tempted to call someone a name, such as walk away; call the person by a new, more positive nickname; or count to ten in their heads. Ask students to brainstorm what they can do the next time they hear someone else call others mean names.

Good Citizen Points

MATERIALS

roll of tickets

ticket jar

Help students learn respect for adults and see them as trustworthy. Give several tickets to staff members and adults that come in contact with your students both at school and in the neighborhood, such as other teachers, the principal, bus drivers, cafeteria workers, playground supervisors, or crossing guards. Ask the adults to give a ticket to one of your students each time they notice him or her being a good citizen. (Be sure to give tickets yourself!) Tickets can be given for following directions, waiting quietly in line, helping others, or performing any other mature, kind action. Have students place tickets in a class jar as they earn them. Determine a number of tickets to be earned by the class. When the class attains their goal, treat them to a movie and popcorn party.

Respecting School Staff

MATERIALS

construction paper

pencils, crayons, colored pencils, markers

Have the class list names of school staff members other than teachers, such as the nurse, custodian, cafeteria workers, or secretary. Invite student groups to make secret-admirer cards for each person on the list. In the cards, have students list why they appreciate the staff members. Ask students to place the cards where staff members can easily find them. On a designated day, invite staff members to class to find out the identities of their secret admirers. Have staff members sit with their groups and discuss the importance of mutual respect as it relates to their jobs.

MATERIALS

objects from nature

Respecting Nature

Bring in an object from nature and explain how a person can respect it. (For example, bring in a leaf. Explain that a person can respect a leaf by planting seeds to grow new trees.) Take students on a nature walk. Have students find objects that need to be shown respect, leaving them in their natural environment. When students are back in the classroom, have them discuss their object and tell how it can be shown respect.

MATERIALS

butcher paper

paper slips

crayons, colored pencils, markers, paint, paintbrushes

Equation Banners

Have students brainstorm several respect equations such as *Kind Words + Calm Temper = Respect* or *Helping Others + A Good Attitude = Respect.* Ask students to write an equation on a paper slip. Divide students into groups of four or five. Have each group choose their favorite equation and write it on a large piece of butcher paper. Have them make a banner, illustrating a scene showing the equation. Invite groups to hang their banners throughout school.

Grandparents' Day

Invite students to share stories about their grandparents. Read aloud a variety of grandparent books. Discuss student reactions to these stories. Invite students to write love letters or draw pictures for their grandparents. Invite students without grandparents to write letters or draw pictures for residents of a local senior citizens center. Send a letter home inviting grandparents and older friends to come to class and share a hobby or story with the class. On the designated Grandparents' Day, have students read their letters, and have grandparents share their hobbies and stories. Engage the class and their visitors in special art projects, sing-alongs, and games.

MATERIALS

books about grandparents such as *When I'm Old with You* by Angela Johnson, *Through Grandpa's Eyes* by Patricia MacLachlan, *The Wednesday Surprise* by Eve Bunting, and *The Sunshine Home* by Eve Bunting

writing paper

drawing paper

crayons, colored pencils, markers

envelopes

R-E-S-P-E-C-T

Divide the class into seven groups. Assign each group one letter in the word *respect*. Write ____ *stands for* _________ on the board. Have students brainstorm a sentence that describes respect and uses their letter at the beginning of the sentence, such as *R stands for resolving problems peacefully*. Have each group write their sentence on paper and think of a way to explain or give examples of its meaning. Have each group design their letter and paint it on a piece of posterboard. Ask the class to spell *respect* by having groups hold up their letters and read and explain their sentences. Invite the class to give respect presentations to other classes.

MATERIALS

writing paper

tempera paint

paintbrushes

seven posterboard pieces

MATERIALS

chart paper

markers

Attention Please!

Ask a volunteer to help demonstrate effective, polite listening. Ask him or her to discuss an exciting summer event. During his or her story, be rude—interrupt the student, ask questions, and comment about similar experiences you have had. Ask students what you did that showed you were not listening politely. Have them identify things you should do to be a good listener. Chart this information. Apologize to the student for being rude, and ask him or her to begin the story again. This time, do not say anything. Instead, squirm, yawn, roll your eyes, and look away from the speaker. When the speaker finishes, announce, *I did what you said. I didn't interrupt. I was a good listener, right?* Have students name the specific actions that demonstrated you were not listening politely. Once again, ask the speaker to begin. This time, do not interrupt. Maintain eye contact, nod, smile, and lean in. When the speaker finishes, ask students how they knew you were listening. Chart this information. Add the headline *Attention Please!,* post the chart, and refer to it frequently during lessons and activities.

MATERIALS

none

Listening with Your Eyes, Ears, and Hearts

Ask students to discuss the body parts we use to listen. (Students will probably say, *ears.*) Explain that, while this is true, the Chinese have a model for listening that says we must use our eyes, ears, and hearts to truly listen. The model explains that when we use these three body parts, we give a speaker our undivided attention. When you need students' attention, announce, *I need your eyes, please.* Teach students to respond, *And our ears and hearts.*

Positive Attitude

an accepting, content outlook

Poster Idea

Enlarge, decorate, and display the following poster to remind students to keep a positive attitude.

Part of learning is facing challenges and making mistakes. Children need to learn that mistakes and challenges are to be expected. These situations are easier to accept when children maintain a positive attitude. In a classroom setting, children with a positive attitude

- focus on the good rather than the bad.
- use positive language to make their point.
- naturally give compliments.
- understand it is okay to make mistakes and try to correct them.
- have dreams for the future and believe they will come true.
- show appreciation for others' efforts.
- give their best effort in every endeavor.
- trust in themselves, their teacher, and their classmates.
- accept diversity in others without trying to change them.

MATERIALS

When I Was Young in the Mountains by Cynthia Rylant

construction paper

pencils, crayons, colored pencils, markers

book-binding materials (hole punchers, paper fasteners)

Focusing on Positive Memories

Invite students to share special times they enjoy with their families. Suggest that everyone has good times and bad times. Explain that some people focus on good memories, while others focus on the bad. Tell the class you want to have a year during which everyone focuses on good experiences. Read *When I Was Young in the Mountains* aloud. Invite each student to draw a picture of a positive memory he or she has from the current month. Have students briefly explain their memories in writing at the bottom of the pictures. Repeat this activity each month of the school year. Save the pictures. At the end of the year, have students create a cover and bind their pictures to make a personal yearbook.

MATERIALS

paper slips

gray construction paper

crayons, colored pencils, markers

shoe box

metal coffee can (optional)

matches (optional)

Saying *Good-Bye* to Put-Downs

On a paper slip, have each student write a hurtful put-down he or she never wants to hear again. Invite student volunteers to share what they wrote and explain why the words hurt. Have students create construction-paper tombstones for the put-downs. Ask students to place the put-downs in a shoe box. Bury the put-down box outside. (Another option is to place put-downs inside a metal coffee can and light a fire inside the can. If you choose this option, check with the administrator first, keep students away from flames, and bring necessary safety equipment. Sprinkle the ashes across the playground.) Display the put-down tombstones in the classroom and discuss what students can do to keep the put-downs from coming back. Implement one or two of the suggestions, posting reminders in the classroom.

Positive Charting

MATERIALS

chart paper

markers

Ask students to brainstorm conditions that enable them to have a good day in class. Chart the responses. Post the chart and refer to it when reminding students what enables everyone in the classroom to be content, comfortable, and safe.

Affirmations

MATERIALS

butcher paper

markers

chart paper

Explain the meaning of the word *affirmation.* Discuss an affirmation you received and how you felt when you received it. Ask volunteers to describe affirmations they received. Form student groups. Give each group a sheet of butcher paper and markers. Ask each group to brainstorm as many affirmations as possible. Provide examples of single-word affirmations such as *Great!,* short-phrase affirmations such as *Way to go!,* and sentence affirmations such as *I love your handwriting!* After ten minutes, invite groups to take turns reading their lists. Record the affirmations on chart paper. Ask students to continue thinking about affirmations, adding any new ones to the list the following day. Post the chart and encourage students to use affirmations when they work in groups. Add new affirmations to the list as students think of them.

MATERIALS

writing paper

Compliments

Distribute writing paper, and have each student write his or her name at the top. Ask each student to pass his or her paper to the student on the right. Invite that student to write a brief positive message about the student whose name appears on the paper. Have students continue passing papers until they receive their original paper. Invite students to quietly read their peers' positive comments.

MATERIALS

Mean Soup by Betsy Everitt

writing paper

Recipe for Recovering from a Bad Day

Ask students to name favorite soups and describe the ingredients. Display the cover of *Mean Soup*. Ask students to predict the ingredients in mean soup. Read the book aloud. Ask each student to write a recipe for how he or she might recover from a bad day. Invite students to share their recipes with the class. Highlight those that solve problems with a positive attitude.

Believing in Your Dreams

Read aloud *El Chino.* Discuss how the character in the book believed in his dream, even though he encountered much adversity. Distribute drawing paper and have students cut out a large cloud. Ask students to draw a dream they have for themselves. Have students write a caption for the drawing, explaining their dream. Ask students to turn their drawings over and write one thing they have to do to make their dream a reality. Punch a hole in the top of their drawings, tie a string to each one, and hang them from the ceiling. Hang a large cloud with the heading *Sweet Dreams Can Come True.*

MATERIALS

El Chino by Allen Say

drawing paper

scissors

crayons, colored pencils, markers

hole puncher

string

Two for One

Whenever a student is caught criticizing a classmate, have the criticizing student give the classmate two compliments for every criticism he or she made. Students will have a great time catching each other—making a game of it takes the sting out of insensitive remarks. Best of all, students quickly learn to exercise self-discipline and maintain a positive attitude when speaking with classmates.

MATERIALS

none

MATERIALS

none

I Appreciate . . .

Invite the class to sit in a large circle. Explain that when people have positive attitudes, they share their appreciation with others. Have each student think of one person in class they appreciate and why. Taking turns, invite each student to complete the sentence *I appreciate ____ because . . . .* When everyone has had a turn, go around the circle and tell each student why you appreciate him or her. Encourage "I appreciate" statements throughout the year.

MATERIALS

lyrics and recording of "What a Wonderful World" by Louis Armstrong

record, cassette, or compact disc player

What a Wonderful World illustrated by Ashley Bryan (optional)

drawing paper

crayons, colored pencils, markers

chart paper

markers

three-ring binder

Looking for Goodness

Play the song "What a Wonderful World." (If available, share the picture book of the same title.) Ask students to brainstorm other things that make this world wonderful. On chart paper, convert the brainstorming suggestions into new lyrics and sing the students' version. Have students find a partner. Have each pair illustrate a different line from the new song. Bind the illustrations into a class book.

See-the-Good Mural

MATERIALS

butcher paper

art supplies (crayons, markers, fabric scraps, beads, glitter, pipe cleaners, sequins, glue, paint)

Hang a long piece of butcher paper across one wall. Have students write *See the Good* across the paper. Invite students to create a mural by designing a large scene that shows the good in society, such as children playing together, neighbors helping each other, beautiful trees and flowers, or an outdoor concert. Have students use art supplies to decorate the mural. Display the mural during Open House or Back to School Night.

I Can't Stand It! Charades

MATERIALS

none

Explain that although everyone has to do things he or she doesn't like to do, it is important to keep a positive attitude when doing them. Ask each student to think of one thing he or she can't stand to do, even though he or she should. Invite volunteers to pantomime what they don't like to do. Ask students to guess what the volunteers are acting out. Afterward, ask questions such as *Why do people sometimes have to do things they don't like? How do responsible people react when they are asked to do something they dislike? How do people show they have a positive attitude when they are doing things they do not like?* To close, invite children to act out things they love to do.

MATERIALS

writing paper

chart paper

posterboard

art supplies (crayons, markers, fabric scraps, beads, glitter, pipe cleaners, sequins, glue, paint)

Make Peace, Not War

Explain that the expression *Make peace, not war* was a slogan during the 1960s. Ask student groups to brainstorm a list of alliterative slogans by substituting other words for peace and war, such as *Make affirmations, not arguments; Make bonds, not belittlements;* or *Make companions, not condemnations.* Invite students to share their lists with the class. Have students choose their favorite slogans and create a class list. Have each student choose a slogan from the class list and make a poster for it. Invite students to display their posters throughout the school.

MATERIALS

chart paper

markers

Words That Feel Good

Before starting a cooperative group activity, ask students to brainstorm synonyms for positive character traits such as kindness or cooperation. Chart the synonyms. Tell students to demonstrate these words as they work with their group. Just before ending group work, ask students to choose a word from the list and use it in a sentence describing one of his or her group members.

Good News

MATERIALS

current newspapers

markers

Divide the class into groups. Invite groups to scan newspapers and circle as many positive articles as possible. Have groups read their favorite article, discuss it, and give an oral report to the class. After all articles are shared, ask questions such as *Are there trustworthy people in society? Does the good that happens in the world overshadow the bad? Why or why not? How would you describe people in the articles? Are you that kind of person?*

Knowing Your Feelings

MATERIALS

Feelings by Aliki

chart paper

markers

Discuss that it is normal to have different feelings and emotions. Emphasize that although everyone expresses his or her emotions differently, it is important to keep a positive attitude and work to change bad feelings. Read *Feelings* aloud. Have students brainstorm positive ways to express each feeling from the book. Make four charts, each with a different heading—*Anger, Sadness, Frustration,* and *Boredom.* Tape a chart in each corner of the classroom. Divide the class into four groups, inviting each to stand near a chart. Give each group three to five minutes to write all the positive ways to deal with the emotion on their chart. After a designated time, have groups rotate clockwise to the next chart. Have each group rotate to and write on every chart. Invite volunteers to read the charts aloud. Display the charts and refer to them so students can learn positive ways to deal with their emotions.

MATERIALS

A Warm Fuzzy Tale by Claude Steiner

writing paper

boxes with dividers

contact paper (optional)

Warm Fuzzy Mailboxes

Read aloud *A Warm Fuzzy Tale* and discuss the story. Emphasize the positive feelings that occur when one receives a "warm fuzzy"—an affirmation or compliment. Have students write "warm fuzzies" to one another. Establish rules such as *Notes must always be positive, using appropriate language and ideas. Notes may only be written after all other work is completed.* Provide mailboxes for students to give and receive notes. Boxes with dividers can be obtained from discount stores, office supply stores, or grocery stores. If you wish, cover the boxes with contact paper and display them in the classroom.

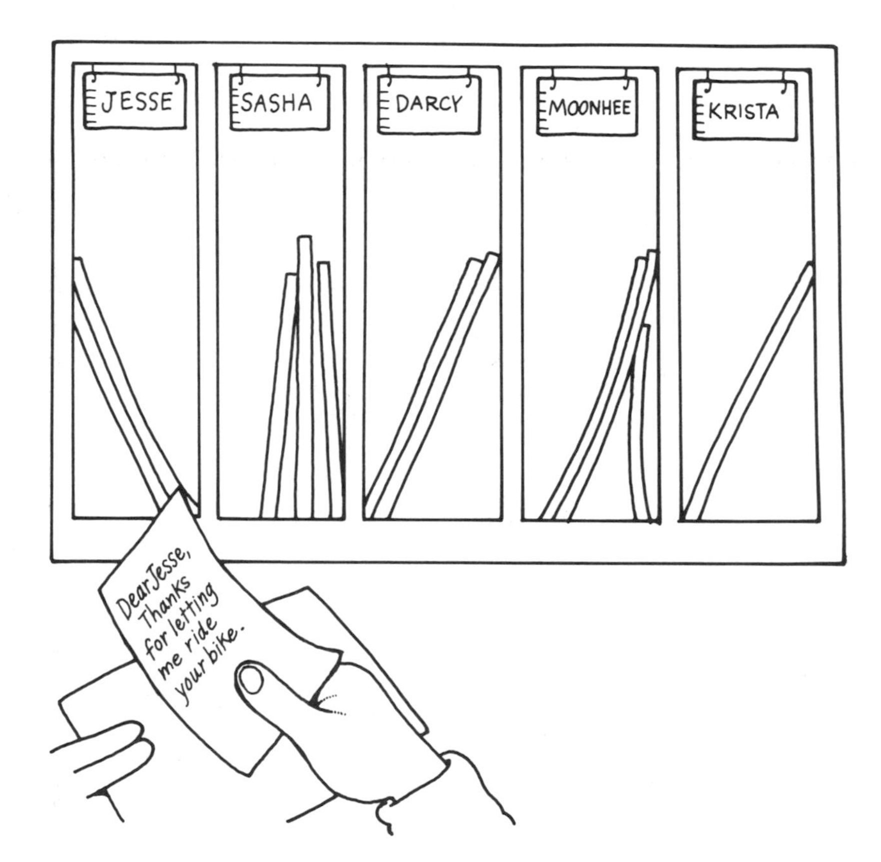

MATERIALS

posterboard

markers

Positive *I* Message

Teach students to use a "Positive *I* Message" when they have a problem. Explain that beginning a sentence with the word *you* places blame on the other person, such as *You make me so angry!* Explain that beginning a sentence with *I* makes a person take responsibility for his or her own feelings, such as *I feel angry when you throw sand on me!* Display the sentence, *I feel ____ when ____* on posterboard so students can refer to it when having problems. Be sure to model Positive *I* Messages when speaking with students.

Conflict Resolution/ Problem Solving

finding solutions in a peaceful, fair manner

Poster Idea

Enlarge, decorate, and display the following poster to help students solve problems peacefully.

One sign of maturity and character development is the ability to peacefully resolve conflicts. When children solve their own problems, a teacher can put his or her referee's whistle aside and provide quality education. When a problem-solving classroom environment is established, children

- compromise when necessary.
- follow teachers' or leaders' directions without complaint.
- resolve conflicts through peaceful discussion.
- work for the common good.
- treat others fairly.
- use kind rather than unkind language.
- accept change.
- openly accept differences of opinion.
- think of others—put themselves "in other people's shoes."

MATERIALS

Grandpa's Face by Eloise Greenfield

drawing paper

crayons, colored pencils, markers

My Face

Read *Grandpa's Face* aloud. After reading, discuss what students might do when worried about someone's feelings and the types of faces they like to see when they are having problems. Give students a piece of paper, and ask them to fold their papers in half. On the left side, have students draw a picture of themselves encountering a problem. On the right, have them draw a picture of themselves working to solve that problem. Have students share their pictures. After sharing, ask discussion questions such as *Would solving your problem take perseverance? How? Why is it important to solve your own problems instead of letting someone else solve them for you? What kinds of faces do you make when encountering a problem? What kinds of faces do you make when you are determined to solve a problem?*

MATERIALS

drawing paper

crayons, colored pencils, markers

Peacing It Together

Distribute drawing paper to each student. Ask each student to draw a large peace sign on his or her paper. In the four sections of the peace sign, ask students to write about or draw how they can create peace by avoiding conflict and positively solving problems. In one section, have them write about or draw how they can create peace in the classroom, such as ignoring rude comments. In the second section, they should write about or draw how they can create peace in school (outside of the classroom), such as playing fairly on the playground. In the third section, they should write about or draw how they can create peace at home, such as doing their chores. In the final section, have them write about or draw how they can create peace through self-discipline in the community, such as riding bikes on sidewalks instead of lawns. Invite students to share their ideas. Display the peace signs under the heading *We're Peacing It Together!*

Following Your Dreams

Read aloud *Uncle Jed's Barbershop*. Discuss how Uncle Jed refused to allow adversities to distract him from his dreams. Ask volunteers to give a description of their personal dreams for the future. Have students role-play situations in which they try to pursue their dreams and are confronted with adversity. Invite students to brainstorm how they might work through the adversities.

MATERIALS

Uncle Jed's Barbershop by Margaree King Mitchell

Dealing with Destruction

Read aloud *Number the Stars*. Explain that many problems in society do not have quick or easy answers. Discuss societal problems that were solved only after much perseverance, such as Apartheid, polio, or women's suffrage. Divide the class into groups of four or five students. Have each group read and discuss a newspaper article. On chart paper, ask groups to list several ways (even though they may require much perseverance) the problem in the article can be solved. Have groups share their articles and possible solutions with the class. As a class, vote for the best solution from each group. Invite each group to write a community or world leader involved with their problem and suggest the solution chosen by the class. Send the letters—you may even get a reply!

MATERIALS

Number the Stars by Lois Lowry

five newspaper articles, each highlighting a different crisis or problem

chart paper

markers

writing paper

pencils, pens

envelopes

MATERIALS

none

The Same Story

Use this activity to teach students to work together and solve their own problems. Whenever two students are in conflict and come to you with different stories, encourage them to talk together for five minutes to agree upon the circumstances of the conflict. Students then have a chance to work together, not against each other. Send the students to a private area to talk. After five minutes, have them report back to you. If their stories are the same, invite the students to shake hands and congratulate them on working together to solve the problem.

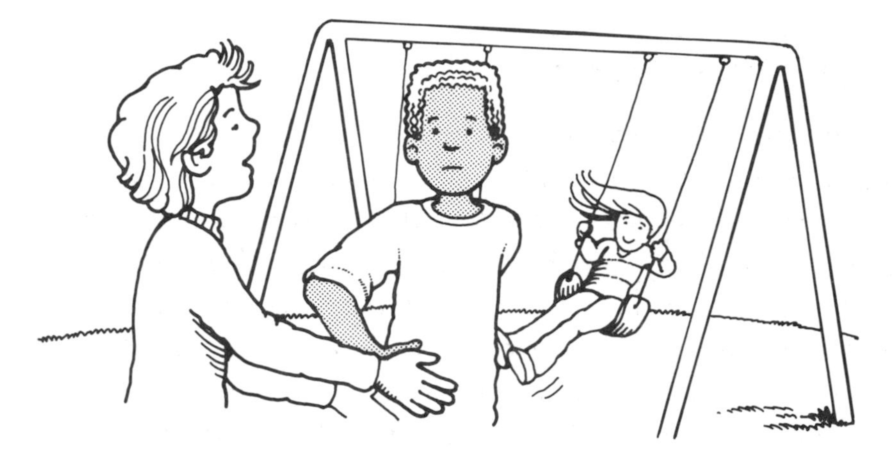

MATERIALS

colored construction paper

biographies of people who worked for peace

Peace Tower

Discuss how several people have devoted their lives to solving problems and creating peace, no matter the cost. Ask students to select and research a peace advocate such as Dr. Martin Luther King, Jr., Menachem Begin, Mother Theresa, Bishop Desmond Mpilo Tutu, Andrei D. Sakharov, Mikhail S. Gorbachev, Albert Schweitzer, Medgar Evers, Mohandas K. Gandhi, Lech Walesa, Jimmy Carter, Woodrow Wilson, Anwar Sadat, Jane Addams, Alfred B. Nobel, or Theodore Roosevelt. Using construction paper, have each student create a one-dimensional "building block" that represents the accomplishments of his or her chosen peace advocate. Students can illustrate or write about obstacles their peacekeepers encountered while trying to achieve their goals. On a bulletin board, mount the construction-paper blocks in a pyramid shape. Explain that the pyramid represents strength—it is strong because, together, the peacekeepers are building blocks that make the world a better place. Use this analogy to explain that every person, no matter who they are, helps the world when he or she works to solve one problem and create peace. Label the bulletin board *Peacemakers Build a Better World.*

Peace Begins with Us

Read aloud *Peace Begins with You.* Discuss students' favorite passages. Ask how students can apply the message of the book to being a peacemaker in their community. Have students brainstorm things they can do in their everyday lives to act responsibly and help maintain peace. Ask students to create simple stories and/or picture books about creating peace. Have students share their stories with other classes.

MATERIALS

Peace Begins with You by Katherine Scholes

writing or drawing paper

pencils, crayons, colored pencils, markers

Being a Dream Keeper

Discuss the work of Dr. Martin Luther King, Jr. Read aloud or play a tape of *I Have a Dream.* Explain that although Dr. King encountered many obstacles, he worked to solve problems in the world. Have students brainstorm how they can solve problems in the world. From student ideas, develop a community service project that helps solve problems for people in need, such as a canned-food drive, participation in a charitable race, or a read-a-thon for which students take pledges. Take photographs of students engaged in the project. Display the photographs around a poster of Dr. King. Ask students to write a reflection of how their involvement in the community service project embraces the goals of Dr. King's speech. Display writings next to the photographs.

MATERIALS

copies or videotape of the speech *I Have a Dream* by Dr. Martin Luther King, Jr.

camera and film

poster or photograph of Dr. King

writing paper

MATERIALS

index cards

construction paper

art supplies (crayons, markers, fabric scraps, beads, glitter, pipe cleaners, sequins, glue)

refrigerator box

Symbols of Peace

Have the class brainstorm several peace symbols such as the peace sign, a white flag, an olive branch, a dove, or two fingers held in a V. Divide students into small groups. Have each group create their symbol using art supplies, and encourage imaginative, elaborate designs. Cut open a refrigerator box so it resembles a partitioned wall. Have students hang their symbols along the wall. Ask each group to create a presentation telling ways they can be living examples of their symbols at school. Invite other classes to view the Wall of Peace and listen to the presentations.

MATERIALS

8" white paper squares

glue

On the Wings of Peace

Discuss the dove as a symbol of peace. Explain that origami is an ancient Japanese art. Distribute a paper square to each student. Have students fold the square in half diagonally and reopen it. Next, have them fold the two uncreased corners of the square in to meet the diagonal crease, resulting in a cone shape. Have students fold up the smaller end of the cone so it meets the larger end. Ask students to fold down the tip of the smaller end to make the dove's head. Have students fold the entire figure in half toward the back, making wings. Direct students to pull out the tip of the smaller triangle until a straight "neck" appears. Have students fold the tips of both wings up to make feet on which the dove can stand. On each wing, ask students to write one thing they can do to solve a problem and create peace. Hang the doves from the classroom ceiling.

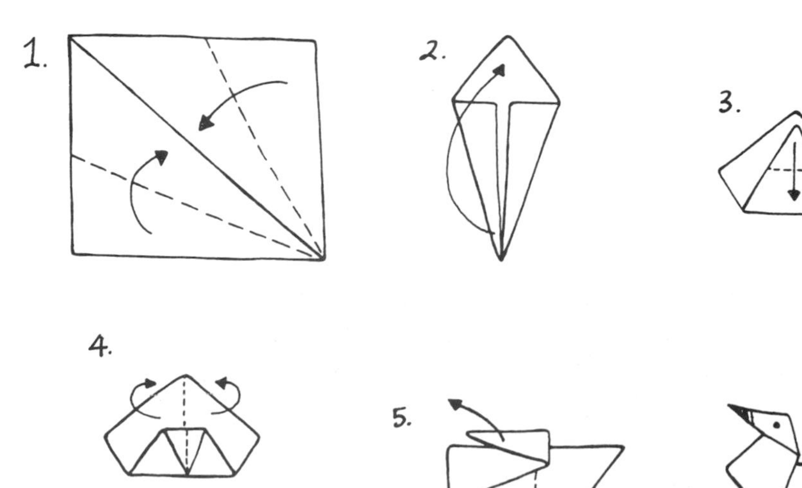

Positive Helping

Use this short "sponge" activity when you have five to ten extra minutes. Read "Helping" aloud. Discuss ways of helping that sometimes are not very helpful at all. Have students use their suggestions and brainstorm ways they can be helpful when people need them.

MATERIALS

the poem "Helping" from *Where the Sidewalk Ends* by Shel Silverstein

Problem-Solving Stories

To help students solve their own problems, have them write problem-solving stories when experiencing conflicts with a classmate. Whenever a conflict arises, have a student fold a piece of drawing paper into fourths, reopen it, and number the boxes one to four. In box one, have the student draw a quick sketch of the problem with a classmate. In box two, ask the student to draw one way he or she can solve the problem. In box three, have the student draw another way he or she can solve the problem. Have the student choose one problem-solving technique and try it. After his or her attempt, have the student use box four and draw the result from trying the chosen technique. Ask the student to write *yes* on the picture if the technique worked, and *no* if it did not. Have the student place the story in a shoe box on your desk. At the end of the week, pull out the story and have a short discussion with the student. Have students write problem-solving stories until conflict-resolution skills have developed throughout the class.

MATERIALS

drawing paper

shoe box

MATERIALS

Alexander and the Terrible, Horrible, No Good, Very Bad Day by Judith Viorst

posterboard outlines of each of the seven continents

pillows or beanbag chairs

Australia

At the beginning of the year, read aloud *Alexander and the Terrible, Horrible, No Good, Very Bad Day.* (This story tells of a young boy who, upon experiencing several bad incidents, decides to move to Australia where he is convinced things are always better.) Divide the class into six table groups. Hang a posterboard continent outline over each group. Hang the Australia outline over an area away from students' seats. Place pillows or beanbag chairs under the Australia outline. Designate "Australia" as a place where students can retreat when they want to escape and spend free time reading, journal writing, or completing other quiet activities. Just like Alexander, students can go to Australia when they are having a terrible, horrible, no good, very bad day.

MATERIALS

none

Ask Three Before Me

Choose times during the school day when you will wait to answer student questions until they have asked at least three peers first. Establish times when the "Ask-Three-Before-Me" policy may be ignored, such as when students have questions about matters of health or safety, or during tests or quiet work time. This policy teaches students that their classmates are valuable sources of information and have many ideas to offer. In addition, this practice allows you to focus on teaching rather than problem solving.

Self-Discipline

controlling of one's own thoughts and behavior

Poster Idea

Enlarge, decorate, and display the following poster to remind students to exercise self-discipline.

When children demonstrate self-discipline in the classroom, they make learning easier for themselves and others around them. A large part of becoming self-disciplined is understanding why it is important. After children understand self-discipline's importance, they need to learn techniques to help them exercise it. Children who exercise self-discipline

- complete their assignments.
- stay on task.
- wait to be called on.
- work toward personal and community goals.
- try again and again.
- ignore peer pressure.
- choose productive rather than destructive activities.
- control their tempers.

MATERIALS

The Cat in the Hat by Dr. Seuss

light blue construction paper

scissors

crayons, colored pencils, markers

What Can I Do?

Read *The Cat in the Hat* aloud. Invite students to discuss how they feel and what they do on a rainy weekend day. Discuss how activities such as watching television or playing video games are fun, but are not always productive. Challenge children to think of productive, self-disciplined activities they can do at home when bored or inside due to rain. Write activities on the chalkboard. Invite each student to choose one thing from the list. Have each student cut a raindrop from light blue construction paper and illustrate what he or she can do on a rainy day. Ask students to write brief explanations for their illustrations. Have students bring their raindrops home and post them as a reminder of what to do on a rainy day.

MATERIALS

writing paper

Activity Log reproducible (page 49)

small prizes (pencils, stickers, free-time passes)

Tune Out T.V.

As a class, brainstorm appealing alternative activities to watching television. Distribute activity logs. Challenge students to avoid watching television for one week. Have students use the log and record the activities they did instead of watching television. Remind students that logs should be signed by an adult. After one week, collect the logs and discuss student experiences. Congratulate and award a small prize to students who went without television all week.

Activity Log

Date	Time From _______ to _______	Activity	Witness

Taking the Work out of Homework

MATERIALS

none

Divide the class into groups. Have each group discuss homework strategies that would make the work more pleasant, such as working with friends or parents, working for several short intervals, snacking while working, or memorizing work to music or rhymes. Have each group share suggestions. Invite students to try one strategy that evening when completing homework. The next day, ask students to share their strategies and tell if the strategies helped their self-discipline and made the experience more pleasant.

Chores

MATERIALS

writing paper

Ask each student to describe the one chore he or she dislikes most. Have students write a letter to their parents promising to complete their chores for one week without complaints. To close the letters, have students ask their parents to write a reply to be read in class at the end of the week. At the end of the week, have students bring in parent replies and read them to the class.

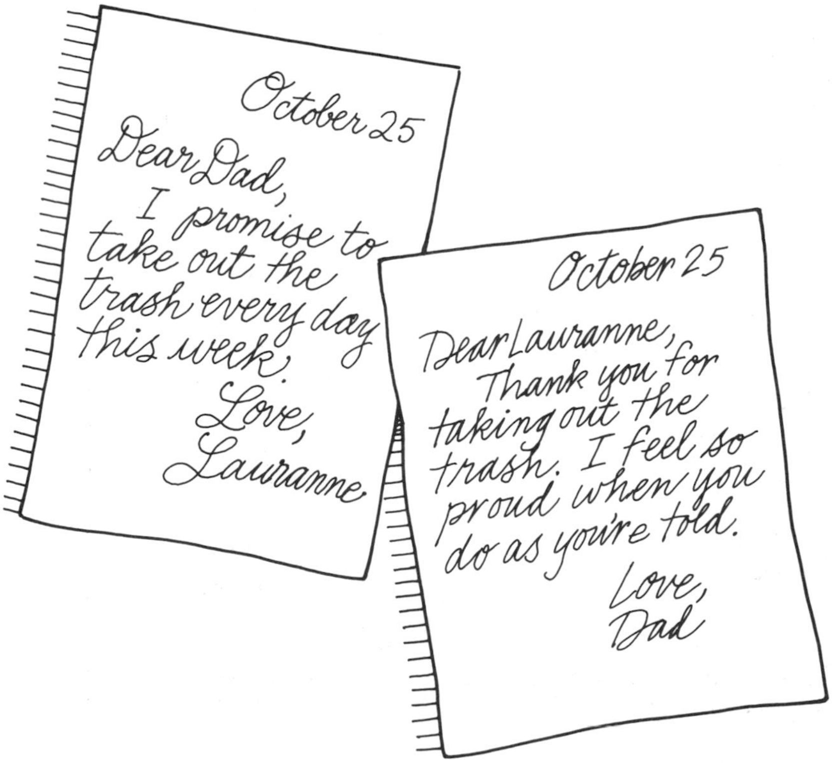

Setting Goals

MATERIALS

paper slips

tape

Invite each student to choose a school-related goal such as *I will raise my hand before talking; I will read during silent reading;* or *I will ask for help when I need it.* Challenge students to choose a goal that he or she needs to achieve rather than an already-attained goal. Have each student write his or her goal on a slip of paper and tape it to his or her desk. For one week, invite students to silently read their goal several times a day and work to achieve it. At the end of the week, have students discuss their results.

Give Me Five

MATERIALS

posterboard

crayons, colored pencils, markers

Have students discuss actions that help them become successful at school. Tell them about five self-disciplined actions to ensure school success. On the chalkboard, write:

1. *Eyes Watching*
2. *Ears Listening*
3. *Hands Still*
4. *Brain Thinking*
5. *Heart Caring*

Discuss the meaning of each action. Invite student groups to make posters that advertise the five actions, and entitle their posters *Give Me Five.* Hang the posters throughout school. Have groups write short commercials to explain their posters. Invite groups to read their commercials over the P.A. system or travel from class to class explaining their posters.

MATERIALS

rope

two small signs (one saying *yes*, the other *no*)

Everyone Else Is Doing It

Stretch a rope along the floor. Place a *yes* sign at one end of the rope and a *no* sign at the other. Tell students you are going to read statements and questions asking them to think about how self-disciplined they are. Tell students if their answers are *yes*, they should move to the *yes* end of the rope and if their answers are *no*, they should move to the *no* end. Explain that if they feel their answers are *maybe yes* or *maybe no* they should move somewhere on the rope between *yes* and *no* as if it were a continuum. Give hypothetical situations such as *Everyone has been stealing gum from the corner store and no one has gotten caught. Would you try it once?* or *Your best friends are smoking cigarettes and offer you one. They call you a chicken for saying "no." They ask again. Would you try just one puff to get them off your back?* Give students time to think and move along the rope. After students have moved each time, choose volunteers from points on the rope to explain their positions. Encourage and praise honesty, even if students are not standing near the "correct" part of the rope.

MATERIALS

list of role-playing sentences

Saying No

In advance, write several dialogue sentences asking a person to do something he or she should not, such as *Do you want to smoke a cigarette?* or *Hey, let's sneak out of the house tonight and go to a movie.* Read each sentence aloud and ask a student to role-play a way to tell you *no*. (Invite students to pass if they cannot think of something to say. Then call on volunteers to answer.) After each response, have the class brainstorm other ways they could say *no* and avoid the bad situation.

What Do I Do When . . .

MATERIALS

8 ½" x 11" paper

Write or type 20 unfinished sentences on a piece of paper. Write thought-provoking sentences that challenge students to think about self-discipline, such as *When my brother or sister calls me a name, I . . . , When I want to do something I know my parents won't like, I . . . , When I'm angry, I . . . , When I have a lot of homework but want to watch a movie, I . . . ,* or *When I am angry with a store clerk, I . . . .* Duplicate and distribute the sentences. Have each student choose a partner with whom he or she feels comfortable. Have student pairs find a private place and take turns finishing the sentences. After each pair has shared, bring the class together. Have students discuss the activity, sharing if they feel they are very self-disciplined, somewhat self-disciplined, or not very self-disciplined.

Try, Try Again

MATERIALS

none

On the chalkboard, write several situations in which a person feels he or she failed, such as *I flunked a spelling test; I made my friend so mad that he or she won't talk to me;* or *I missed the winning goal in soccer.* Read each sentence aloud. Invite students to discuss the problem and brainstorm ways a person could remedy the situation or prevent it from happening again. Invite students to share personal experiences and what they learned from them.

MATERIALS

writing paper

One Thing I'd Like to Do Well

Have each student write one thing he or she would like to do well. Students may choose any skill, such as one that is sport-, school-, or hobby-related. Invite students to choose partners. Have each student work with his or her partner to make a list of small tasks (that take 15 minutes or less) that can be done each day to develop his or her skill. Challenge students to use their lists every day for one week. Each day, remind students to try something from their lists. At the end of the week, have students share and tell if their skills have improved. Invite volunteers to demonstrate their skills.

MATERIALS

file-folder labels

paper

masking tape

plastic wrap

tagboard strips

Crystal Ball

Have students brainstorm what they want to have, do, and be in 20 years. Ask them to write each goal on a file-folder label. Have students crumple paper into a round ball and tape it securely. Have students stick their labels to the balls and then cover the balls with three or four layers of plastic wrap. These are "crystal balls" that see into the future. Invite each student to use a tagboard strip and write three things he or she needs to do to make the goals come true. Have students bend the tagboard into a loop and tape the ends to make a crystal-ball stand. Have students place their crystal balls on the stands, share their goals, and explain what they need to do to make them come true.

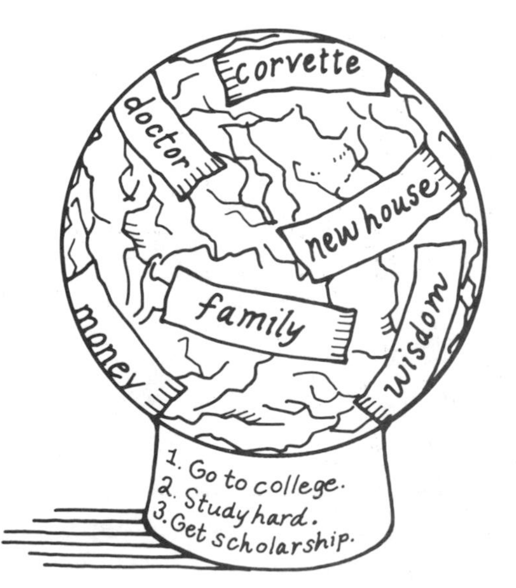

Cooperation/ Teamwork

willingly working with others toward a common goal

Poster Idea

Enlarge, decorate, and display the following poster to remind students to cooperate and work together.

In many cases, children learn best when they learn from each other. For children to work together and learn from their peers, they have to cooperate and work like a team. "Team players" are children who

- listen.
- encourage their peers.
- allow and invite others to contribute their talents and skills.
- follow as well as lead.
- recognize their strengths and use them for the common good.
- treat others equitably.
- recognize the needs of the group.
- think before acting.
- communicate calmly.
- put competition aside.

MATERIALS

student-helper schedule

Helping Out

At the beginning of the year, set up a student-helper program with the school librarian, custodian, lunch servers, and/or playground supervisors. Ask each student to choose a staff member to help, and sign up for a day and time on a schedule. Over a period of weeks or months, have students work with their assigned staff members. After all students have helped, invite volunteers to tell what they liked and disliked about the job and how they felt helping someone with their work.

MATERIALS

two 12"-long fabric scraps

Grab the Tail

Take students outside and divide them into two teams. Have each group form a line. Ask students to hold onto the person's waist in front of them. Have the last student in each line hang a fabric scrap from his or her back pocket or pant waist. Have the first person in each line try to take the scrap from the opposing team. It is each student's responsibility to watch carefully so he or she can act in both a defensive role, such as twisting to get away from the other team, and an offensive role, such as turning toward the other team. After the game, have students discuss how the game required teamwork. Ask questions such as *Think about the game—how did it require teamwork? How can we show teamwork when we work in groups in class? How can we show teamwork in physical education? on the playground? after school?*

Talk on Paper

Frequently invite students to talk about current topics of study. As students become orally proficient, show them how to "talk on paper." Divide the class into pairs and instruct them to share one piece of paper. Instruct one student to write a message and then pass the paper and pencil to his or her partner. The partner then reads the message, writes a response, and passes the paper and pencil back to the first student. Continue this pattern for a set amount of time.

MATERIALS

writing paper

Build It

In advance, build a simple structure from building blocks and place it in a cardboard box. Divide students into groups. Distribute building blocks to each group. Choose an observer from each group to look at the structure in the box. Choose messengers to deliver instructions to each group. Have observers explain what the structure looks like to the messengers. Ask the messengers to relay the information back to his or her group so they can begin constructing what they understand the original structure looks like. (The observer should not be able to see what constructors are doing.) If constructors have any questions, they must ask the messenger to relay the questions to the observer. After all groups finish, have them display their creations and discuss similarities and differences before displaying the original structure. Have the class discuss their frustration in trying to build the structure and relaying messages. Ask questions such as *Did this activity require cooperation? How?* (following directions, listening) *Which activities at school require cooperation? Was the game frustrating at times? Did you show cooperation when you were frustrated? How?*

MATERIALS

cardboard box

Legos or building blocks

MATERIALS

small twigs or craft sticks

piece of ribbon

Sticking It out Together

Collect twigs approximately the circumference of your thumb or use craft sticks. (Gather twice as many twigs/sticks as students.) Give each student one of the twigs/sticks and ask him or her to snap it in half. Be sure everyone experiences success. Tell students that you have another set of twigs/sticks equal in number to those just distributed. Tie the twigs/sticks together. Challenge each student to break the bundle. When everyone has tried (and failed), explain that your classroom is just like the twigs/sticks—when you work as individuals against one another, you can be easily broken. However, when you work as a group, no one can cause you or your classmates to break. Discuss cooperation and teamwork. Give specific examples of times when students did and did not cooperate in groups.

MATERIALS

recorded music

record, cassette, or compact disc player

Friends Stick Together

Have students move around the classroom while you play lively music. Stop the music randomly and call out, *Friends Five!* (or *two, eight,* or any number smaller than the size of the class). Upon hearing the number, have students quickly join together to form the appropriate number, without making a sound or touching anyone. If the number called does not divide students evenly, have extra students stand near you in a group. After several rounds, discuss how the game took teamwork and cooperation. For example, it takes cooperation to maneuver around the room and not touch a person or object and find the correct number of people. Discuss school situations in which students must exercise cooperation and teamwork.

Supporting Each Other

MATERIALS

none

Take students outside. Have them form a circle, standing shoulder to shoulder. Have everyone turn a quarter-turn to the right. Tell students that their toes should touch the heels of the person in front of them. If not, they should slowly move in toward the center of the circle until they do. Tell students to lightly hold the shoulders of the person in front of them. On the count of three, have each student slowly sit in the lap of the person behind him or her. After students have been sitting for a few seconds, tell them to slowly rise on the count of three. (Students may fall down a few times before they succeed, but that's part of the fun!) Discuss that this exercise demonstrates that, through cooperation for the sake of the group, your class can overcome any individual differences you might have. For example, you just supported each other regardless of differences in body weight.

Blob Tag

MATERIALS

pylons

Take students outside and form a large circle. Create boundaries with pylons. Choose two students to come to the center of the circle and be "the blob." On the count of three, have the two students clasp hands and chase other students while they run away. Their hands must remain clasped at all times. If they tag someone, that person joins "the blob" and clasps the hand of one of the "blob" students. When the blob grows to four people, it can separate down the middle to become two smaller blobs. Continue the game until all students have been tagged. After the game, have students discuss how it took teamwork to run the same speed as those with whom they were holding hands. Compare the teamwork required in this game to that required when working with others. Have students give teamwork examples.

MATERIALS

cardboard strips

Shark Attack

Take students to an open playing area, and divide them into groups of eight. Give each group a piece of cardboard just big enough for all group members to stand on. (The cardboard represents a boat.) Have each group stand at one end of the playground. When you yell, *Go!,* students run forward, trying to reach the other side of the playground. As they run, each group member must help carry the cardboard. When you yell, *Sharks!,* students must immediately drop the cardboard and all group members must stand on it. If one member falls off, that group must go back to the beginning and tear a chunk from their boat. After a team successfully reaches the other side of the playground, have students discuss how cooperation was necessary to hold the cardboard, stay on the boat, and help the team. Compare the cooperation required in the game to that required in everyday living. Invite students to share times when they had to cooperate to "keep afloat."

MATERIALS

resources (encyclopedias, reference books, computers)

treats (pencils, stickers, free-time passes)

Quest of the Week

Think of a difficult question such as *If the population of the United States grows by six million people a year, what will the population be in the year 2007?* or *How many Democrats and Republicans are there in Congress?* On Monday, write the question on the board and divide the class into groups. Challenge groups to work together to find the answer and think of a creative way to report the information to you (such as a poster, poem, or skit). Tell students if they present the answer by Friday afternoon, they will receive a treat. If the class answers the question and works together on the presentation, give each student a treat.

Class Goal

MATERIALS

class money jar

At the beginning of the year, have the class choose a place they would like to visit, such as a special event, zoo, park, or restaurant. Determine the cost of admission and transportation for the whole class. Report the cost to the class, and explain that you will arrange the trip if they can earn the money to attend. Invite the class to brainstorm ways to earn money, such as selling things, offering services, or conducting a pledge drive. Throughout the year, hold fund-raising events. Have volunteers count the money once a month. When the class has earned the money, take them on the trip.

Up a Tree

MATERIALS

gift-wrapped box

treats (candy, pencils, stickers)

Place treats in a gift-wrapped box. Place the box in a tree or other high place. Tell the class that there are treats for them in the box if they can get the box down. Explain rules for retrieving the box: *No one's feet may leave the ground. No person may touch the box until it reaches the ground. Any item or combination of items in the classroom may be used to retrieve the box, but they may not be thrown or broken.* Invite students to brainstorm ways to get the box down. Invite students to choose and try three methods for retrieving the box. When the box comes down, pass out the treats. To complete the activity, ask questions such as *How did this activity require teamwork? Is it easier or more difficult to persevere with others' help? Which classmates offered others the most encouragement? Did encouragement help the group meet its goal?*

MATERIALS

none

Human Knots

Divide the class into groups of eight to ten students. Have students in each group stand in a circle, shoulder to shoulder. Ask everyone to reach out with their right hands and take someone else's hand. Then ask everyone to reach out with their left hands and take a different person's hand. Challenge students to untangle and become a circle without unclasping hands. (Students will have to twist, turn, and climb over and under each other to untangle.) After the activity, discuss how it took cooperation to untangle. Ask questions such as *Did your group ever feel like giving up or cheating? What stopped you? Did everyone in your group show the same level of cooperation? How could you tell?*

MATERIALS

yarn ball

Everyone Counts

Have students stand in a large circle. Give a yarn ball to a student. Have the student tell one thing he or she can do to overcome bad things in society. After the student shares, have him or her hold the yarn at the end of the yarn ball, and toss the ball to another student so the two students are connected by a piece of yarn. Continue this process until every student has spoken and a large yarn "spider web" has been made. Explain that the web symbolizes that everyone must do his or her part to hold things together and make the world a better place. Through cooperation and teamwork, terrible things can disappear and wonderful things can be achieved. Ask five or six students to let go of their yarn. (The web should collapse.) Explain that the web now symbolizes that without teamwork, we cannot achieve our hopes for the world.

Drawing Together

Have each student find a partner. Give each pair a piece of drawing paper and one crayon. Explain that partners will hold one crayon together and draw a picture. Tell students they may not talk before or during the activity. For three to five minutes, play classical music in the background as students draw. When the music ends, have students stop drawing. Invite partners to share their drawings. Discuss reactions to the activity, highlighting the role cooperation and teamwork played in the drawings' outcomes.

MATERIALS

drawing paper

crayons

classical music recording

record, cassette, or compact disc player

Concentration

Have students sit in a large circle. Assign a number to each student, keeping number one for yourself. Establish a four-count rhythm in which students slap their legs, clap their hands, snap their right fingers, and snap their left fingers. On the right finger snap, call out your number (one). On the left finger snap, call out a student's number (such as nine). The person whose number you call then repeats his or her number on the next right finger snap and calls another number on the left finger snap. (The person responding may not call out the number of the person who just called his or her number.) Continue playing until someone breaks the rhythm. When that occurs, have the person who missed go to the last spot in the circle, having everyone move up a number. The goal is for each student to have his or her number said in one round of play. After several attempts, discuss the concept of cooperation and how it relates to the game. Ask questions such as *What was the common goal in this game? How does it feel to rely on others to meet a common goal? How does it feel when someone makes a mistake and cannot help meet the common goal? What can we do to encourage others to succeed when we're working as a group?*

MATERIALS

none

MATERIALS

lunch bags

wrapped food items (bananas, sandwiches, cookies, cheese, crackers)

Pack a Lunch

Divide the class into equal teams. Have each team sit on the floor in a line. Give the first player on each team an empty lunch bag and food items. (Explain that the food should not be destroyed and the bag should not be torn during the game.) At a signal, have the first players put each item in the lunch bag, one at a time, and pass it to the second players. The second players should remove all the items and pass them and the empty bag to the third players. The bags move down the rows of players, being emptied and refilled until they reach the end of the lines. After the game, have students discuss how it took cooperation to complete the game. Discuss mealtime at home and why it is important to cooperate when a family member is preparing food. To close, invite each team to divide and eat the lunch.

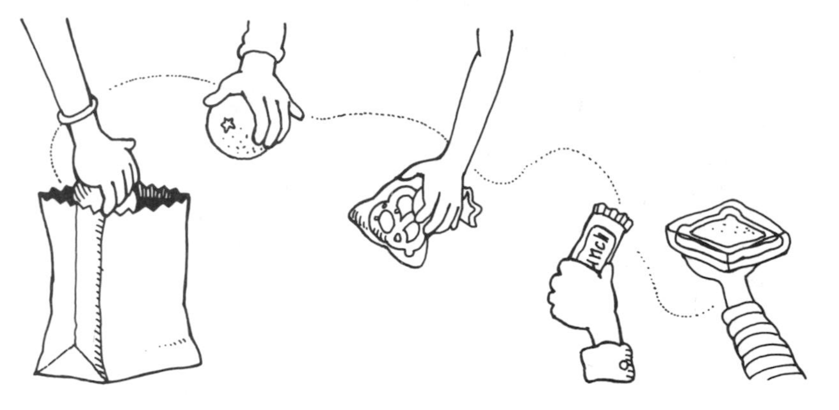

MATERIALS

masking tape

Draw-a-Face Relay

Divide the class into equal teams. Use masking tape to make a starting line approximately six to eight feet from the chalkboard. Draw a large box on the chalkboard for each team. Have teams stand behind the starting line. At a signal, have the first players walk to the chalkboard, draw a person's head in the box, and return to their teams, handing the chalk to the second players. Have the second players go to the chalkboard and draw two eyes. Have third players draw a nose, fourth players draw a mouth, fifth players draw two ears, and sixth through eighth players draw individual hairs on the head. To help students remember what they should draw, invite them to remind their teammates. When the relay is complete, discuss how teamwork and cooperation were important in this game. (Team members had to remind teammates and pay attention.) Discuss how reminding others and paying attention helps when working in cooperative groups at school.

Friendship

accepting, giving, sharing, feeling, and enjoying companionship with others

Poster Idea

Enlarge, decorate, and display the following poster to remind students to be good friends.

Children naturally seek friends like themselves. The challenge is to help children find friendship with those different from themselves, such as those of a different gender, race, personality type, stature, or mental- or physical-ability level. Children who become friends with others, regardless of differences, make the classroom a comfortable, happy place to be.

Children who are good friends

- accept others for who they are.
- share their belongings.
- listen.
- enjoy others' company.
- support others in need.
- smile, laugh, and tell jokes.
- avoid teasing and put-downs.
- encourage others with kind words.
- avoid tattling.
- ask for help from their peers.
- solve problems peacefully.
- consider others' feelings before acting.

MATERIALS

lyrics and recording of "You've Got a Friend" by James Taylor

record, cassette, or compact disc player

writing paper

You've Got a Friend

Distribute song lyrics and play "You've Got a Friend" for the class. Invite students to sing along if they wish. Have students pretend someone wrote the song for them and ask, *Who is that kind of friend to you? Why do you deserve a friend like that? If you wrote that song, who might you write it for? Why?* Have students write answers to the questions. Divide the class into groups and have students share their answers. (If you wish, use the song to open Friendship Circle, page 9.)

MATERIALS

writing paper

black construction paper

small, colored paper squares

fine-tipped markers

glue

I'm a Good Friend

Ask students to discuss times when they were good friends to others. Have them explain what they did to show friendship. On writing paper, have students list qualities possessed by someone who is a good friend. On black construction paper, ask students to sketch an outline of something they believe symbolizes friendship, such as a smiling face, a birthday party, or holding hands. Have students fill in the sketch with small paper squares to make a mosaic. Invite each student to write a quality from his or her list on the design by writing a letter in each mosaic square. Have students share their work. Display the mosaics on a bulletin board entitled *Quality Friends, Friendly Qualities.*

Broken Heart Race

Use this activity as a way for students to make friends at the beginning of the year or to find partners for activities. Make a paper heart for each pair of students. Cut each heart into two-piece puzzles, making each puzzle different. Place the puzzles in a paper bag. Have each student choose a heart piece. At a signal, ask students to search for the one who can mend their "broken heart." When students find their partners and match their puzzle pieces, have them sit next to each other. When all partners are sitting, distribute a prize to everyone.

MATERIALS

paper hearts

scissors

paper grocery bag

prizes (pencils, stickers, free-time passes)

Be a Rock

Early in the school year, read aloud *Everybody Needs a Rock.* Take students outside and ask each to find a special rock. When you return to class, have each student write his or her name on a paper slip and place it in a container. Have students choose a name from the container. Ask students to use paint pens or markers to print the name they picked on top of their rocks and their own names on the bottom. Have the class sit in a circle. Invite students to present their rocks to the people they chose and tell how they can be a "rock" for them in class. For example, a student may offer help with reading. Display the rock collection in a special place in the classroom.

MATERIALS

Everybody Needs a Rock by Byrd Baylor

rocks

paper slips

small container

paint pens or permanent markers

MATERIALS

none

Friend to Friend

Pair each student with a partner. Call a direction such as *Hand to hand!* At the command, all students touch hands with their partners. Call another direction such as *Elbow to elbow!* This time, all students touch elbows with their partners. Continue calling similar directions. Finally, call, *Friend to friend!* At this command, have students shake hands with their partners and quickly run to a new partner. Begin with new commands.

MATERIALS

none

Have You Seen My Friend?

Take students outside and have them form a circle. Ask one student (Player A) to run around the outside of the circle and stop behind a student (Player B). Have Player B ask, *Have you seen my friend?* Have Player A reply, *What does your friend look like?* Player B then describes a student in the circle. When the described person recognizes him or herself, he or she begins chasing Player B, trying to tag Player B before he or she can run around the outside of the circle and get back to his or her own place. If Player B is tagged, he or she goes back to his or her spot in the circle and the game begins again. If Player B gets back to his or her place in the circle without being tagged, the chaser (described person) becomes Player A and the original Player A takes a place in the circle.

How to Win Friends

Read aloud *How to Lose All Your Friends.* Divide students into small groups to list ways they can win friends. Discuss lists as a class and compile a master list. Follow the format of the book and turn the list into a story entitled *How to Win Friends.* Write each line of the story on a separate piece of drawing paper. Give each page to a pair of students to illustrate. Compile pages into a three-ring binder and add the book to your class library.

MATERIALS

How to Lose All Your Friends by Nancy Carlson

drawing paper

crayons, colored pencils, markers

three-ring binder

Friendship Bracelets

Have students choose three different-colored yarn pieces. Pair students with partners. Have each student tie his or her yarn pieces together in a knot at one end. Have one partner hold the other's yarn while he or she braids the three pieces together until the braid is approximately nine inches long. Have students tie another knot at the end of the braid. Ask students to trade positions so the other partner can braid his or her yarn into a friendship bracelet. Invite students to give their friendship bracelets to their partners and tie the bracelets around the recipients' wrists.

MATERIALS

24" yarn pieces (different colors)

MATERIALS

stuffed toy insect

writing paper

safety pin

small tote or travel bag

Travel Bug

Discuss the size and scope of the world's population. Explain that while we may not know everyone in society, there are many good people in the world. To learn about the friendliness of others in the world, have students send out a "travel bug." In September, have the class compose a letter telling about their class and giving directions for taking care of the travel bug. For directions, write information such as *Please write a note and tell us about yourself and where you're from. If you wish, pin something to the travel bug or place a postcard or small object in his bag. Then give the travel bug to someone who is going on a trip and ask him or her to read this letter and follow the instructions. If you receive the travel bug on or near May 1, please return the travel bug to . . . .* Invite a student to give the travel bug to someone going on a trip. Place the travel bug in a tote or travel bag and send the bug on his way. At the end of the year, when the travel bug is returned, read the letters and learn about friendly people from around the world.

MATERIALS

none

Buddies

Discuss why it is important to be friends with young children. For example, younger children need positive role models and can learn a lot from older friends. Arrange for your class to help a kindergarten class on a regular basis. Pair each kindergarten student with a student from your class. One day a week, have both classes work together on art projects, science experiments, or physical-education activities. Have older buddies help younger buddies complete their tasks.

Honesty/Trust

being sincere, truthful, trustworthy, and loyal

Poster Idea

Enlarge, decorate, and display the following poster to remind students to be honest and trustworthy.

Honest is something you are. Trust is something you have. Although they are different character traits, honesty and trust are interrelated. Children trust others when they are honest. In turn, children tell the truth when they trust. Demonstrated in the classroom, honest, trusting children

- tell the truth despite consequences.
- voice their opinions in a kind, thoughtful way.
- "tell on" someone only when necessary.
- show and share their feelings.
- know their classmates and teacher care and want the best for them.
- feel and react without guilt.
- express themselves positively as well as critically.

MATERIALS

index cards

markers

How Do I Rate?

Have students write numbers one through five on index cards, one number on each card. Tell students you will ask them to react to statements and secretly rate themselves by looking at a card. Explain that card number one stands for the lowest ranking and card number five stands for the highest ranking. (If students feel they are in the middle, they should look at number three. If they feel they are somewhere in between, students should look at card two or four.) Read statements such as *I am never afraid to tell the truth; I am a good friend; I am a good brother or sister; I am a good son or daughter; I am a good grandchild; I am a good student;* or *I am a good citizen.* After each statement, have students look at the card showing their ranking. After all statements have been read, repeat the activity and have students publicly rate themselves by *holding up* their cards. Have students think about any changes that occurred in two sets of rankings. Discuss if it was difficult to be honest when students knew others would see their answers compared to when they were rating themselves secretly.

MATERIALS

writing paper

On the Job

Invite students to go home and interview three adults about their jobs. Have students ask two questions: *How does your job require honesty?* and *How does your job require trust?* Have students record their answers. Invite students to share their findings, telling the occupations of the people and how they use honesty and trust in their jobs.

I Cannot Tell a Lie

MATERIALS

chart paper

markers

Discuss the legend in which George Washington chops down a cherry tree and confesses. Ask students to share a time when they were tempted to lie to stay out of trouble. Choose one student's situation and write it on the chalkboard. Make a two-column chart on chart paper. At the top of the left column, write *Consequences for Lying*. At the top of the right column, write *Consequences for Telling the Truth.* Have students brainstorm possible consequences for lying or telling the truth in the situation listed on the board. Ask students to consider the consequences, put their heads down, and raise their hands if they would tell the truth in that situation. Share the vote tally with the class and discuss the outcome.

Consequences for Lying	Consequences for Telling the Truth
· GROUNDED	· GET YELLED AT
· NEVER GET TO GO TO HIS HOUSE AGAIN	· APOLOGIZE
· FEEL GUILTY ALL THE TIME	
· HAVE TO PAY FOR IT	

Six Feelings

MATERIALS

six large signs, each with a name of one of the seven dwarves from *Snow White* (excluding Doc)

After a rigorous activity or an extended break from school, display six signs, each with a name of a dwarf (Happy, Sneezy, Bashful, Dopey, Grumpy, and Sleepy). Ask students to choose the name they most feel like at that moment. Explain that it is okay to be honest about what they are feeling. Have students cluster around the sign that describes their feelings. Once students are in groups, give them approximately 15 minutes to create a skit dramatizing their emotions. Invite each group to perform their skits for the class.

MATERIALS

blindfolds

Trust Walk

Have each student find a partner. Ask one student in each pair to put on a blindfold. Ask sighted partners to silently lead their blindfolded partners to a predetermined place such as the playground slide, and back. Have the sighted partner lead by taking their sightless partner by the arm; no talking is allowed. When students return, ask them to reverse roles and repeat the activity. Invite students to reflect on the experience and what they learned about trust.

MATERIALS

Report Card reproducible (page 75)

Personal Report Cards

Just before parent/teacher conferences, have students complete a personal report card. Carefully explain each question, reinforcing the importance of honesty to oneself. (Some questions may bring chuckles from students. It's fun for students to discover who they are and what they do, even when it's less than perfect.) Before collecting report cards, have students write *yes* on the top of their card if they want it to be shared at parent/teacher conferences and *no* if they do not. Ask students to think about why they chose *yes* or *no*. Ask questions such as *Did you say* no *because you were honest or dishonest? Did you say* yes *because you were honest or dishonest?* After conferences, return cards to students who wrote *no*, and invite them to share the cards at home.

Report Card

Answer each question with *yes, no,* or *sometimes.*

Do I . . .

- get in trouble? ____________
- get my work done on time? ____________
- respect the property of others? ____________
- work hard? ____________
- listen? ____________
- talk when someone else is talking? ____________
- make noise? ____________
- clean up after myself? ____________
- improve my grades? ____________
- write neatly? ____________
- tip my chair frequently? ____________
- help my teacher? ____________
- fight? ____________
- throw things? ____________
- keep a neat desk? ____________
- read during free time? ____________
- follow directions? ____________
- try my best? ____________
- use my time wisely? ____________
- like school? ____________
- come to school clean and neat? ____________
- participate in class? ____________
- check my work? ____________
- respect others? ____________
- take care of school property? ____________
- steal? ____________
- talk back to teachers? ____________
- hurt people's feelings? ____________
- lose my temper? ____________

Am I . . .

- friendly? ____________
- creative? ____________
- naughty? ____________
- nice? ____________
- quiet? ____________
- hard-working? ____________
- patient? ____________
- late for school? ____________
- in control of myself? ____________
- sloppy? ____________
- honest? ____________
- fair? ____________
- careful? ____________
- cooperative? ____________
- responsible for my actions? ____________
- a "tattle tale"? ____________
- self-disciplined? ____________
- caring? ____________
- a "team player"? ____________
- fun to be with? ____________

MATERIALS

none

Courthouse Trip

Arrange a visit to a local courthouse and a meeting with a judge. Before arriving, explain to the judge that *honesty* and *trust* are the focus of the trip. Ask the judge to explain the roles that honesty and trust play in the judicial system, such as the honesty required of witnesses and the trust the public must place in juries and judges. Have students tour the courthouse, listen to the judge's presentation, and if possible, observe court proceedings in action.

MATERIALS

chart paper

markers

Telling Them with Tact

Discuss the meaning of the word *tact* and how being honest does not mean being mean or rude. Write situations on chart paper. Divide the class into groups, and have them consider each situation and think of tactful ways to inform the person of his or her circumstance. Bring the class together, and have each group share its solutions. Throughout the year, remind students to be honest, and at the same time, use tact.

Responsibility

being dependable, self-disciplined, and trustworthy

Poster Idea

Enlarge, decorate, and display the following poster to help students develop a sense of responsibility.

As children get older, we expect them to become more and more responsible. If we have high expectations for children, they learn to take responsibility and meet them. Children feel empowered when expected to succeed—they take responsibility because they see new tasks as privileges. In the classroom, responsible children are those who

- understand and accept consequences for their actions.
- complete assignments.
- clean up after themselves.
- do the "right thing."
- tell the truth.
- help others in need.
- complete a task without being asked.
- follow through without giving up.
- understand the effect they have on others.
- try to correct their mistakes.
- apologize (and mean it).

MATERIALS

dollar bill

Where's the Dollar?

Before students return to class from recess, place a dollar bill on the floor. As students enter, stand near the dollar, but do not say anything. Watch student reactions. When students are seated, pick up the dollar and ask them what they would have done if you were not standing nearby or if they found it on the sidewalk. Ask students what they would do if they found a hundred or a thousand dollars. Ask questions such as *How would your actions change if the amount of money was large or small? Should you keep the money if no one asks for it? Should you turn it in if it's a small amount? Should you keep the money if someone asks for it? Should you tell him or her you don't have it? Do you have a responsibility to the person who lost the money? If so, what?* Encourage honest discussion without judging or reprimanding students for differing opinions.

MATERIALS

variety of props

videotape and camera

Home Alone

Discuss the movie *Home Alone* and how the main character protected himself. Have students discuss unrealistic situations that make this movie a fantasy. Invite students to discuss real-life things they can do to protect themselves if they spend an evening or day alone. Have students discuss household safety as well as safety from intruders. Divide the class into groups. Invite each group to create a skit that details one safety tip. Have students use props to make their skits more realistic. Videotape the skits to make a series of "Home Alone" public-service announcements. Have the class write an introduction and follow-up to their videotape and present it to other classes.

I Can Do It!

MATERIALS

writing paper

Have students brainstorm and list things their parents still do for them that they could do themselves, such as make beds, do laundry, pick up toys, find shoes, or cook meals. Have each student choose one item from his or her list and write a parent letter asking for permission to do that thing for a week. At the end of the week, have students give oral reports detailing their experiences, successes, and obstacles.

Privileges

MATERIALS

writing paper

Discuss the concept of privileges as it applies to responsibility. Divide the class into groups. On the chalkboard, write *If I'm responsible when I ______, I ______. If I'm irresponsible when I ______, I______.* Ask student groups to complete a pair of sentences for each of five actions (for example, *If I'm responsible when I do my homework, I get to stay up late. If I'm irresponsible when I do my homework, I get grounded.*). Have each group share their lists. After groups share, have students discuss why responsible people are often given privileges irresponsible people are not. Ask questions such as *Are there advantages to being responsible? What are they? Why do adults trust some children more than others? What do adults think of children who are irresponsible? What do friends think of other friends who are irresponsible? What can you do to become more responsible?*

MATERIALS

drawing paper

crayons, colored pencils, markers

Doing Your Part

In advance, draw a three-paneled picture (triptych) on the chalkboard, showing how people act responsibly at home, in the community, and in their country. Label the sections *My Family, My Community,* and *My Country.* Discuss the concept of responsibility and how we all have do our part to help make the world a better place. Ask students to create their own triptychs, drawing a scene in each panel that illustrates what they can do to act responsibly in each situation. When students finish their drawings, hold a Class Responsibility Summit. Ask students to share their drawings and explain how they are taking responsibility to improve the world.

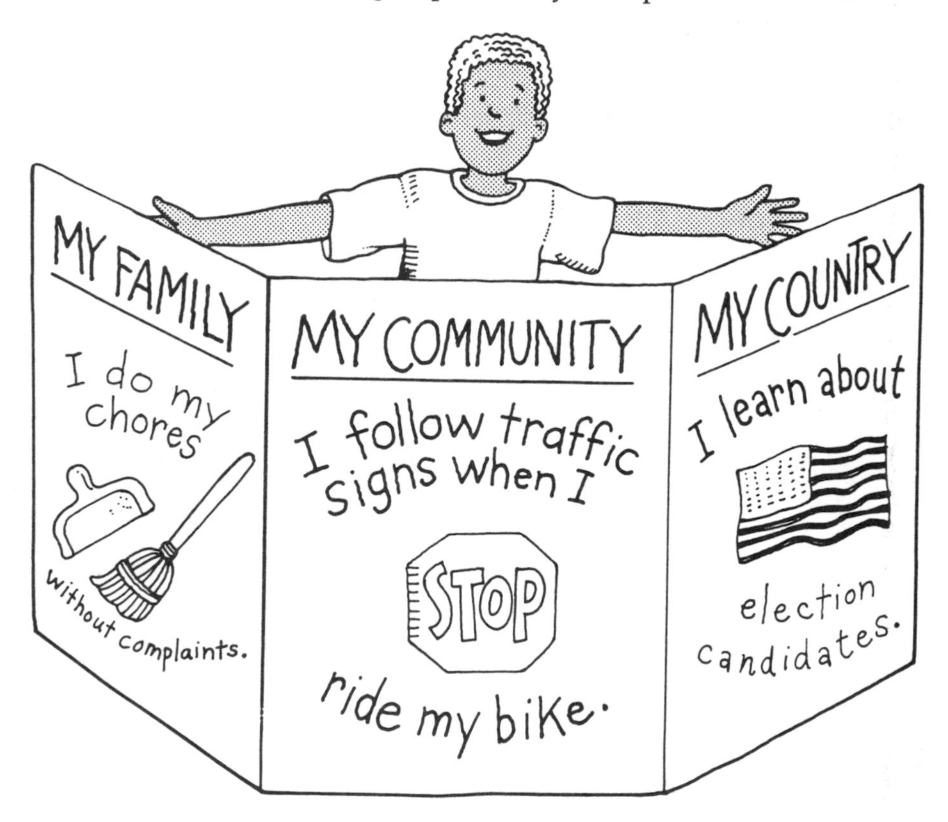

MATERIALS

Contract reproducible (page 81)

Write a Contract

Have students brainstorm things about which they need to be more responsible. If some students are having difficulty with ideas, invite volunteers to offer suggestions. Discuss the purpose of contracts. Divide the class into pairs. Have each student complete a Contract reproducible and have it signed by his or her partner. Ask students to keep their contracts with them at all times as a reminder of their responsibilities. After a two-week period, have students report their progress and tell if the contract helped them become more responsible.

Contract

I, ____,

will try to be more responsible when

____

____

____

____

____

____

____

____

Signed:

____

Witness:

____

MATERIALS

4" x 6" index cards

crayons, colored pencils, markers

No Excuses!

Have each student make an index-card sign that says, *No Excuses!* For one week, have students listen carefully to each other. Challenge each student to make a tally mark on his or her card each time he or she hears someone give an excuse to avoid taking responsibility for something. At the end of the week, discuss the scores, and ask questions such as *Instead of making excuses, what would a responsible person do to correct a situation? How often do you make excuses at home? at school? How do you feel when someone gives you an excuse? Why?*

MATERIALS

none

Homework Club

Designate one day a week to hold a Homework Club. Invite students to stay after school to complete and get help with their homework. After a few weeks, invite students to form their own homework clubs that take place in each other's homes. If you wish, schedule visits to the homework clubs once a month to maintain enthusiasm.

Class Recycling Center

MATERIALS

four large boxes

markers

Write *paper, plastic, aluminum,* and *glass* on each of four boxes. Place the boxes near the wastebasket. For one week, have the class toss their recyclable refuse into the recycling boxes. Keep the waste throughout the week. At the end of the week, have students compare the contents of the wastebasket to the four boxes. Discuss landfills and recycling. Ask discussion questions such as *How can people be more responsible with their garbage? What can you do to help? What are the benefits of recycling? Why don't businesses work harder to create recycled products? How might ecologically-responsible people help the world in the future? Are humans responsible for the well-being of the earth? Why or why not?*

Making Up for Mistakes

MATERIALS

none

On the chalkboard, list several situations in which people make mistakes, such as accidentally taking something from a store, running over a neighbor's toy with a bike, or losing borrowed mittens. Read each situation aloud, asking students to think about what he or she would do in those situations. Discuss the courage it takes to tell someone something he or she may not want to hear or to spend time or money to replace something or help hurt feelings. Have students consider each situation and brainstorm ways to remedy them.

MATERIALS

none

Playground Safety

Complete this activity at the beginning of the year. Divide the class into as many groups as there are pieces of playground equipment. Assign a piece of equipment to each group. Invite students to think of ways to explain and demonstrate the safe use of their equipment. On a designated day, invite younger classes to rotate to each piece of equipment and learn how to use it safely.

MATERIALS

And Still the Turtle Watched by Sheila MacGill-Callahan

drawing paper or posterboard

crayons, colored pencils, markers, paint

The Earth Needs Me

Read aloud *And Still the Turtle Watched.* Discuss student reactions to the book. Ask students to create posters explaining ways people can protect nature in their community, such as not littering, riding bikes instead of using cars, and recycling. Have students think of places in the community where their posters can be displayed. Obtain permission and display the posters.

Compassion/ Kindness

empathizing with others and acting on those feelings with care and concern

Poster Idea

Enlarge, decorate, and display the following poster to help students show compassion and kindness.

Compassion for others, friends or strangers, is a character trait everyone needs. When children feel compassion and express it through kindness, they make themselves better people and the world a better place. Kind, compassionate children

- recognize and express appreciation for others' talents and skills.
- put others' needs before their own wants.
- help others because they want to, not because they have to.
- listen and provide a "shoulder to cry on."
- show kindness without expecting rewards.
- tell and show others they care.
- share.
- recognize and help those less fortunate than themselves.

MATERIALS

hat

paper slips with students' names

Secret Pals

Invite students to draw a classmate's name from the hat. Explain that the name drawn will be that student's secret pal. For a week, have students demonstrate at least two acts of kindness for their secret pals each day. One of these acts should be explicit so it might be recognized by the receiver, such as putting a positive message in his or her pal's warm fuzzy mailbox (see page 38). The other act should be hidden and go unnoticed, such as hanging up his or her secret pal's coat. At the end of the week, have secret pals reveal their identities and share their acts of kindness.

MATERIALS

writing paper

Random Acts of Kindness

Discuss the meaning of *random acts of kindness*. Give examples you witnessed in the classroom. Each day, have students make a list and write short descriptions of random acts of kindness they performed. At the end of the week, have each student read his or her list and share the random act of kindness of which he or she is most proud. Be sure to commend everyone for their actions.

Manners Day

Discuss public courtesy and how it relates to kindness. To demonstrate common courtesy, have a Manners Day. Using plates, utensils, and napkins, model how to set the table and use table manners. Show students how to hold doors for others. Invite students to practice polite telephone greetings and conversations. Have children discuss other ways to show kindness to others.

MATERIALS

plastic plates and utensils

napkins

two toy telephones

Penny Drive

At the beginning of the school year, choose an organization that helps the needy, such as Unicef or The Salvation Army. Invite a representative from the organization to come in and explain the organization's purpose, and discuss why it is important to help and respect those in need. Challenge students to collect pennies, bring them to school, and deposit them in a large jug or bottle. (Send a letter home informing parents of the activity.) At the end of the year, have students count and roll the pennies. Invite the representative to return, speak about the organization's progress that year, and receive the pennies from the class.

MATERIALS

large jug or bottle

pennies

MATERIALS

Honor Badge reproducible (page 89)

crayons, colored pencils, markers

scissors

tape

ribbon

The Greatest Person on Earth

Ask students to discuss people they personally know and admire. Have each student choose one person to honor as *The Greatest Person on Earth*. Distribute honor badges. Ask students to brainstorm the person's positive attributes. On the badge, have students list or draw reasons why their person is the greatest. Have students decorate and cut out their badges. Tape ribbon to the bottom of the badges, as shown. Invite students to give badges to their recipients and explain why they are the greatest people on Earth.

MATERIALS

newspaper and magazine articles about homelessness

Fly Away Home by Eve Bunting

Venn Diagram reproducible (page 90)

writing paper

Empathizing with the Homeless

Share articles with the class about homelessness. Read aloud *Fly Away Home*. Distribute the Venn Diagram reproducible to each child. Invite students to use the Venn diagram to show how they are alike and different from the bird and boy in the story. Have students brainstorm what they can do to help the homeless, such as volunteering in a soup kitchen, placing an artificial evergreen tree in the school office on which to place donated mittens and hats, or having an ice-cream sale and donating the proceeds to a local shelter. Implement at least one suggestion. After the activity, have students write reflections about their experiences and tell what they can do next.

Honor Badge

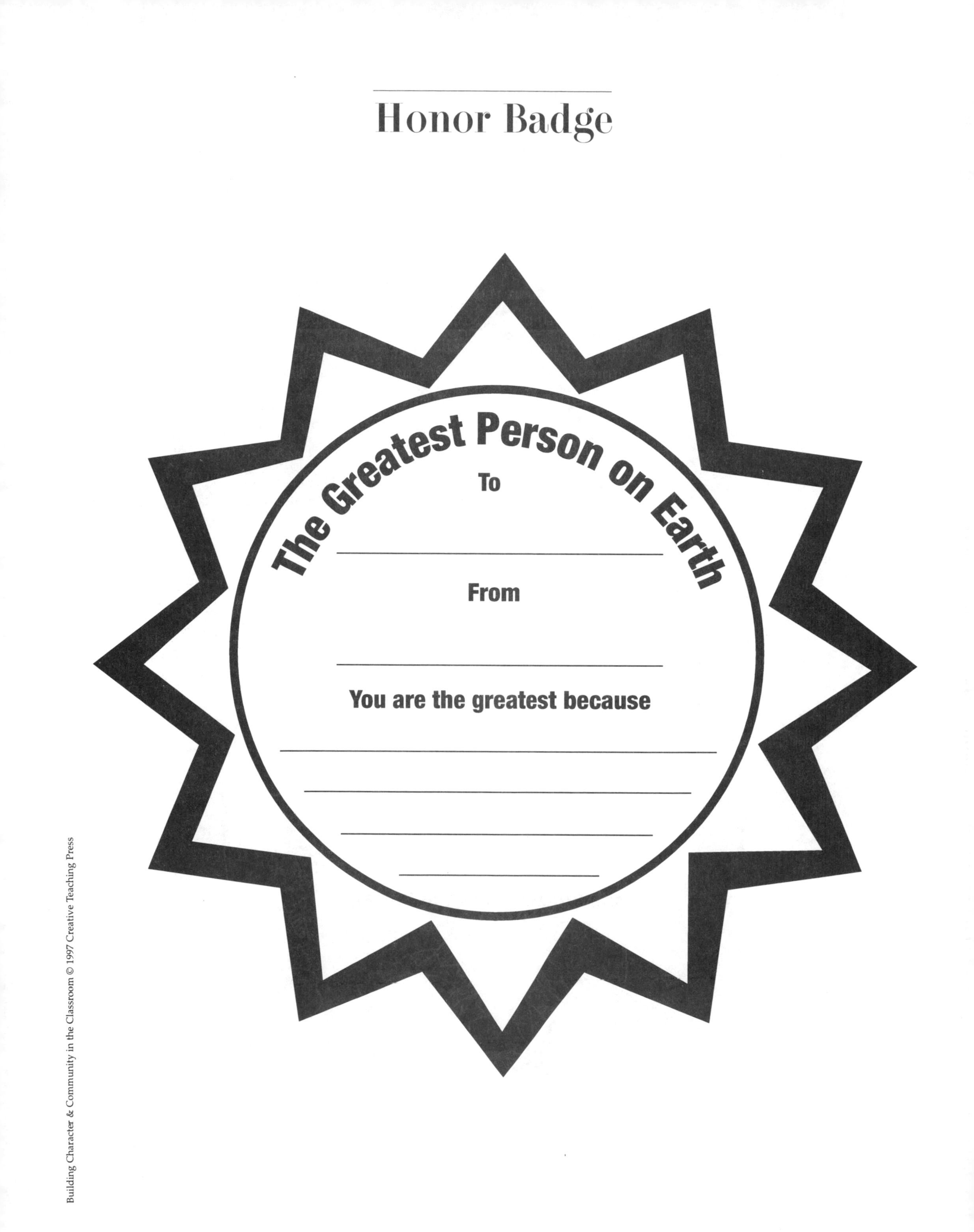

The Greatest Person on Earth
To
From
You are the greatest because

Venn Diagram

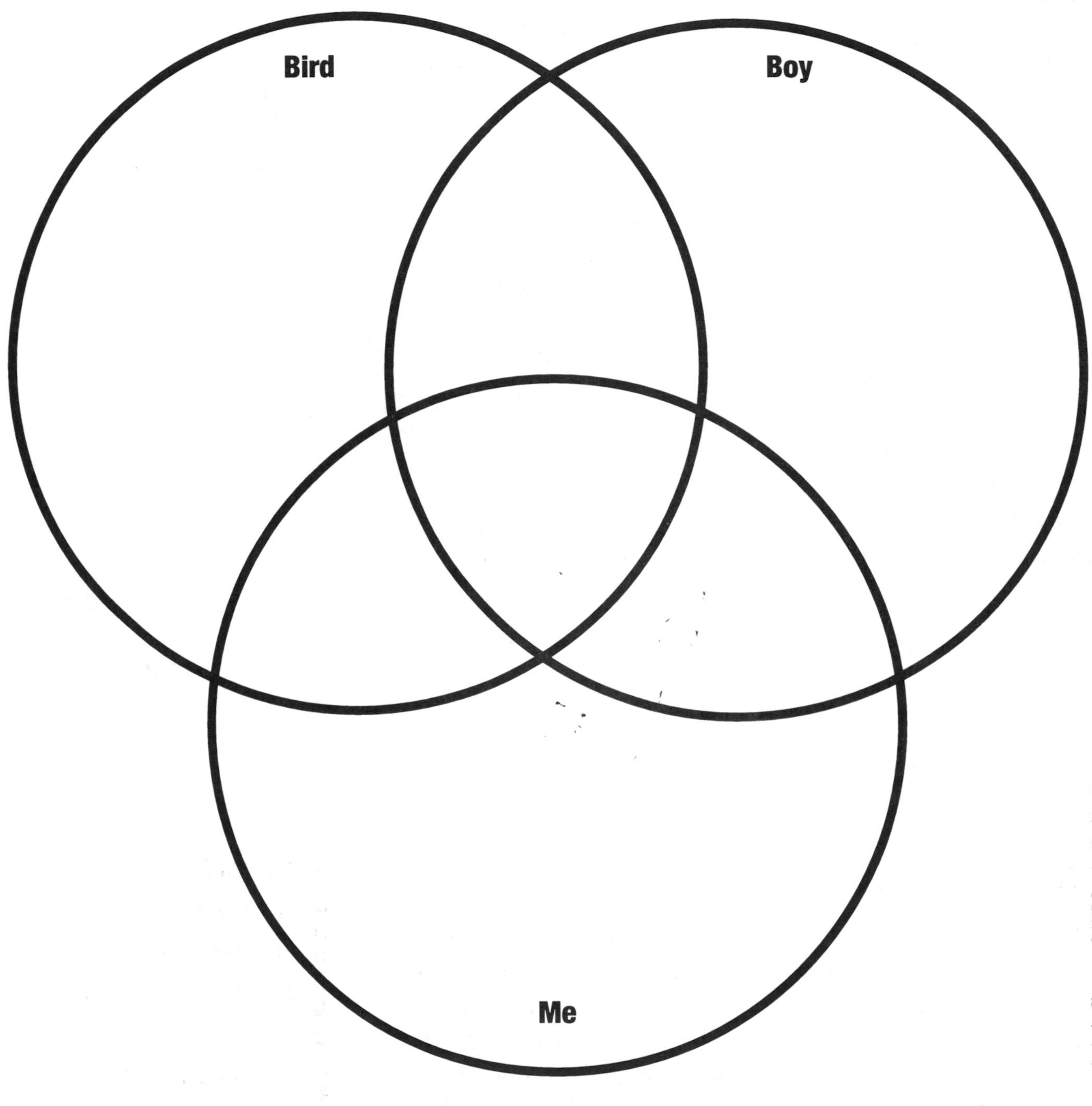

Secret Surprise

MATERIALS

none

Invite each student to plan a secret surprise for the class. Students can bring in anything—a treat for each student, a present for the whole class (such as a movie or guest speaker), or a special poem or book about kindness. Give students a list of inexpensive or free suggestions so everyone can participate. Ask students to inform you of the surprise at least one week in advance. Keep track of who shares a secret surprise, encouraging every student to contribute.

Cookie Exchange

MATERIALS

colored frosting

plastic sandwich bags

paper slips with students' names

lunch bag

large, round sugar cookies

scissors

Place small amounts of frosting in small plastic sandwich bags. Divide the frosting bags into five groups, with each frosting color in each group. Have each student choose a name slip from a paper bag. Divide the class into five groups and distribute cookies and frosting sets to each. Have students snip a corner from the bottom of each frosting bag. Invite students to squeeze frosting from the bags to decorate a cookie for the person whose name they chose. (Encourage students to make cookies they themselves would like to eat.) When cookies are decorated, have students exchange them, and eat.

MATERIALS

writing paper

Neighborly Behavior

Divide students into groups according to where they live, grouping together students who live near each other. Have each group plan one nice thing they can do for their neighbors, such as pick up litter, spend an hour playing with younger children, or do yard work for neighbors or in public areas. Give students a time limit for task completion. Ask each group to write an action plan stating what will be done, by whom, and when the task will be completed. After each group completes their task, have them report back to the class. Ask questions such as *How did doing something nice for others make you feel? Did your neighbors show appreciation for your friendly gestures? How? Will you continue to do nice things for your neighbors? Why or why not?*

MATERIALS

lyrics to two or three songs

drawing paper

crayons, colored pencils, markers

Share a Song

Teach the class to sing two or three songs, or ask a music teacher to share songs from music class. Contact a local nursing home and arrange a time for the class to visit and present the songs. Invite students to make cards for residents of the nursing home. On the day of the visit, have students present the cards to the audience and sing songs. Upon returning to school, discuss why it is important for us to remember and care for people in nursing homes or other health-care facilities.

Field Trip

MATERIALS

clipboards with writing paper or notebooks

Contact a philanthropic organization such as The American Red Cross, The Lion's Club, The United Way, or The American Heart Association. Arrange a field trip to the organization's headquarters. (If a field trip cannot be arranged, invite a guest speaker to the class.) Before the trip, have students write three questions they would like to ask organization staff. Invite students to carry clipboards or notebooks, ask questions during the tour, and write down the answers. After the field trip, ask discussion questions such as *How does this organization help people? Why do people choose to help strangers? Why are organizations like this necessary? What could you do to help people other than your family and friends?*

Coupon Book

MATERIALS

8 1/2" x 11" paper

crayons, colored pencils, markers

stapler

Ask students which shows more caring and kindness, completing a task your parents ask you to do or completing a task *without* being asked. Have students explain their answers. Have students fold a piece of paper into fourths and cut it into four pieces. Ask students to staple the papers together to make a small book. Have them brainstorm several special favors they can do for their parents, such as wash the car, make breakfast, or rake the yard. Write suggestions on the chalkboard. Ask students to choose four good deeds and make a coupon for each. Have students design and draw a coupon on each page of their books. Invite them to bring the books home and present them to their parents to be redeemed whenever their parents choose.

MATERIALS

none

Who Heard a Good Idea?

Anytime students complete work in small groups, have them report what they heard. Instead of asking, *Who has a good idea?,* ask, *Who heard a good idea?* or *Who heard something interesting?* By having students frequently answer these questions, several benefits emerge. Students' listening and cooperative skills improve. They have a wonderful opportunity to model kindness. Creativity increases as outgoing students share creative ideas from the more introverted, reflective thinkers. Speaking skills improve because sharing others' rather than their own ideas tends to be less intimidating.

MATERIALS

planter

tree branch

construction-paper leaves

markers

tape

Good Deeds Tree

Plant a large branch in a planter and place it in the classroom. Provide construction-paper leaves in a central location. Ask students to write a description or draw an illustration of a random act of kindness shown to them on the paper leaves. Tape the leaves to the branch. Encourage students to write on leaves whenever they observe a classmate doing something nice for them or someone else. Invite students to tape the leaves on the tree. Discuss how the more the tree grows, the more caring the class becomes.

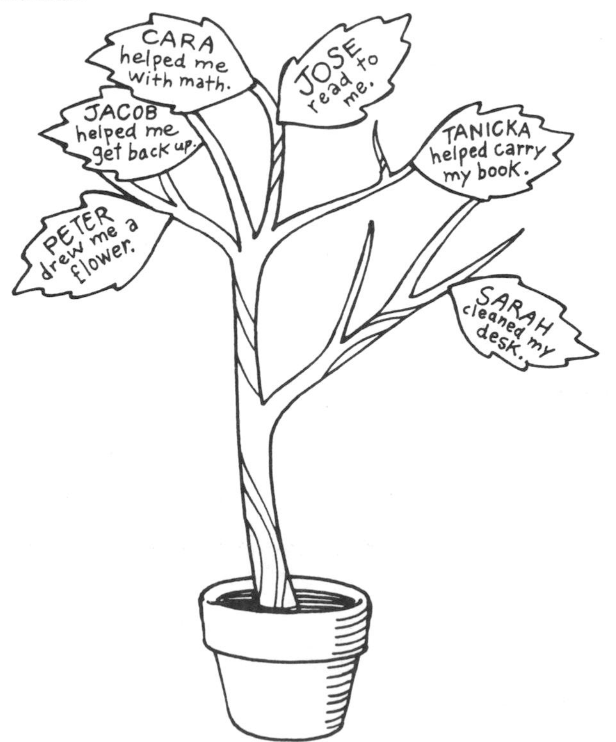

Positive Message Board

MATERIALS

butcher paper

markers

Designate one bulletin board as a positive message area. Cover the bulletin board with butcher paper. Instruct students to use markers and write (directly on the butcher paper) any compliments they would like to publicly share. Be sure to frequently add your own positive messages to the board.

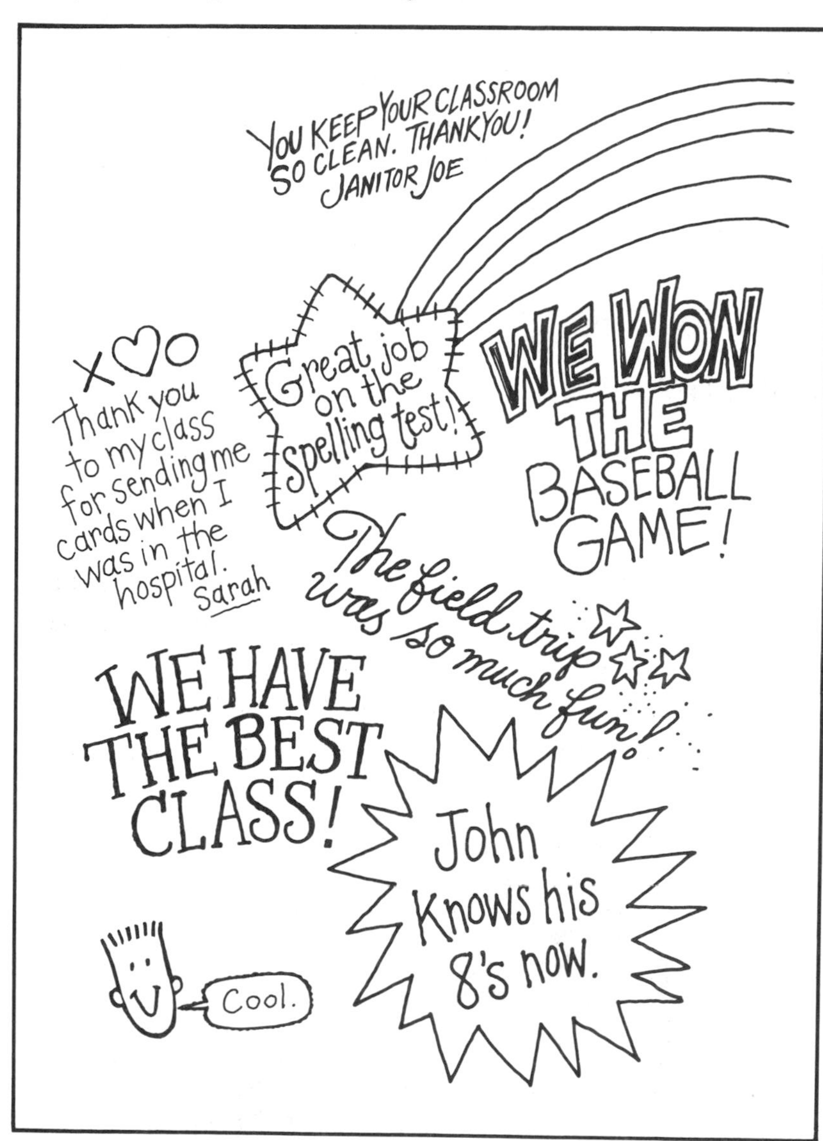

Caring Words

MATERIALS

sentence strips

markers

As a class, brainstorm words that convey compassion such as *love, caring, cooperation, understanding,* and *patience*. Write words on sentence strips. Each day, display one of the words on the chalk tray. Ask students to give examples of times when they saw a classmate exhibit this behavior. Challenge each student to put the word into action sometime during the day. At the end of the day, ask each student to report his or her actions.

MATERIALS

writing paper

Dear Ms. Kindness

On the board, write a "Dear Abby" letter that details a problem regarding compassion, such as

> *Dear Ms. Kindness,*
>
> *I just got glasses and am afraid to wear them because I know everyone will call me "four eyes." What can I do?*
>
> *Sincerely,*
>
> *Can't See but Don't Care!*

Divide the class into groups. Have each group imagine they are Ms. Kindness and write a response. Invite groups to share their letters, and have the class discuss what they liked about each.

MATERIALS

none

Kindness Day

Have each student choose one person he or she sometimes treats unkindly, such as a brother, sister, or friend. Challenge each student to choose one day that week and be kind to the chosen person all day. Along with general acts of kindness, ask each student to do one special thing for the person, such as doing one of his or her chores or helping him or her with homework. At the end of the week, invite students to share their experiences. Discuss if kindness was returned and reactions of the chosen people.